EASY PIANO

THE IRISH COLLECTION

ISBN-13: 978-1-4234-2872-5
ISBN-10: 1-4234-2872-2

HAL•LEONARD®
CORPORATION
7777 W. BLUEMOUND RD. P.O. BOX 13819 MILWAUKEE, WI 53213

In Australia Contact:
Hal Leonard Australia Pty. Ltd.
4 Lentara Court
Cheltenham, Victoria, 3192 Australia
Email: ausadmin@halleonard.com

Visit Hal Leonard Online at
www.halleonard.com

ARTHUR McBRIDE

Traditional Irish Folk Song

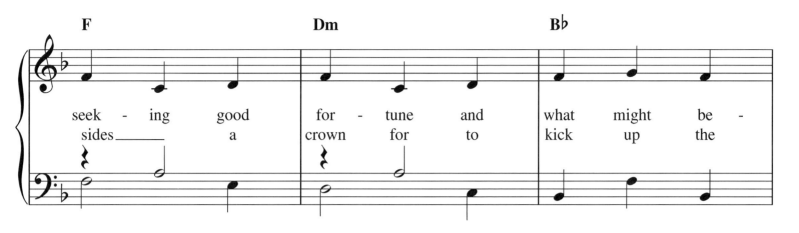

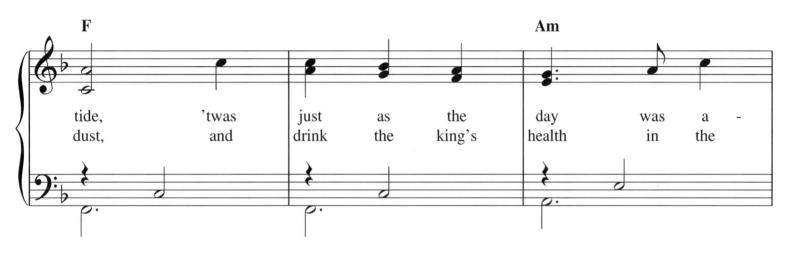

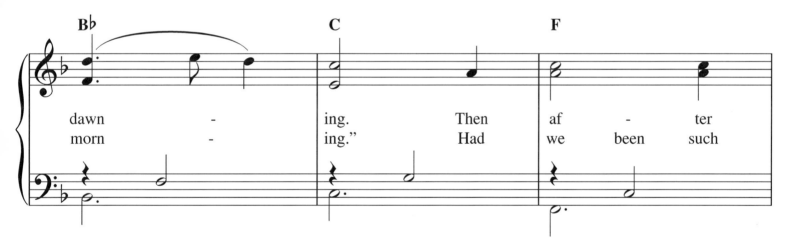

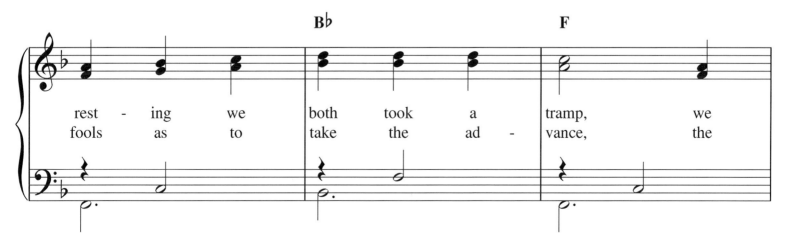

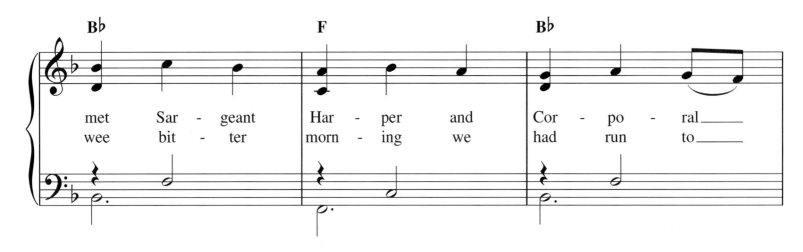

met Sar - geant Har - per and Cor - po - ral____
wee bit - ter morn - ing we had run to____

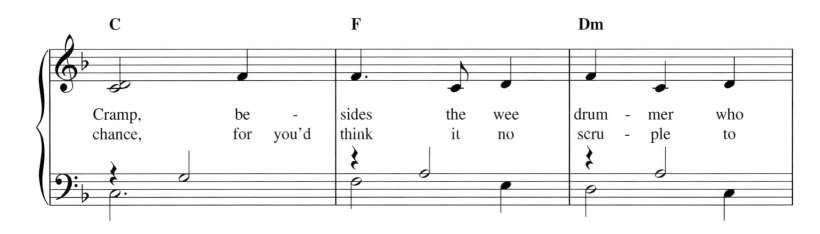

Cramp, be - sides the wee drum - mer who
chance, for you'd think it no scru - ple to

beat up for camp, with his row - dy - dow -
send us to France, where____ we would be

dow in the morn - ing.
killed in the morn - ing.

BOLD FENIAN MEN

Traditional Irish Melody
Words by M. SCANLAN

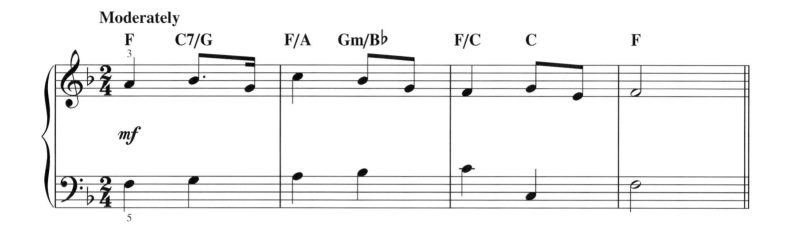

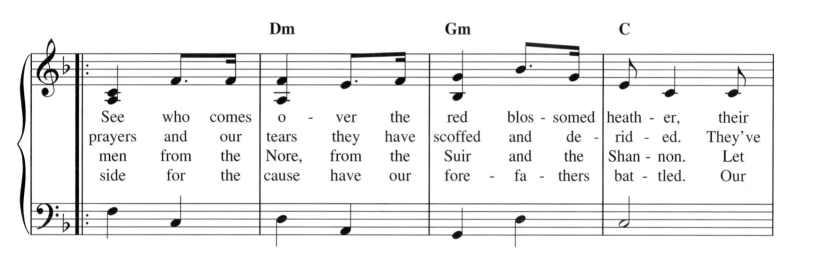

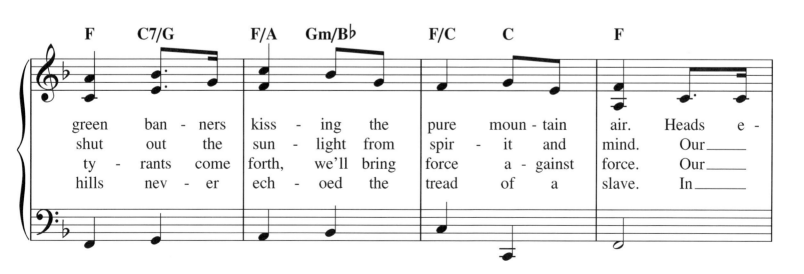

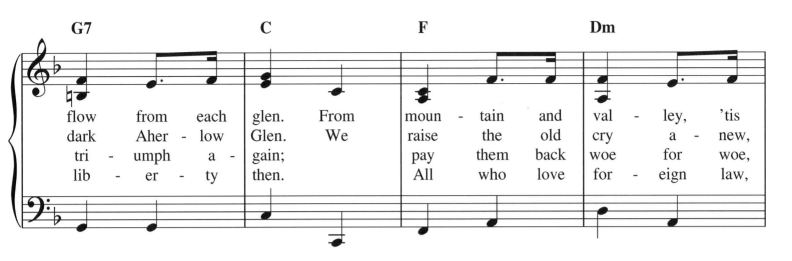

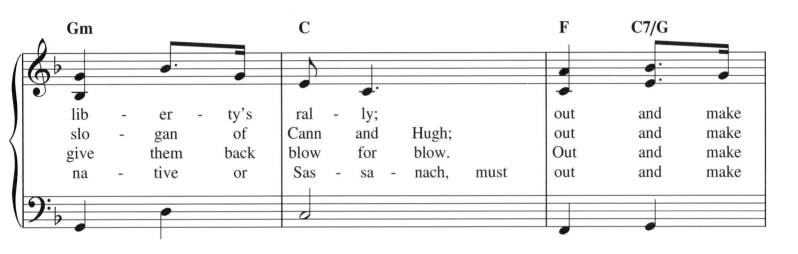

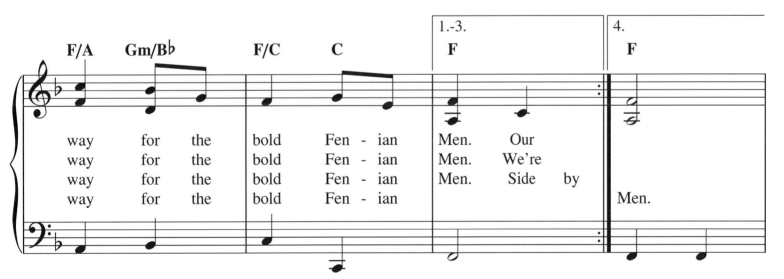

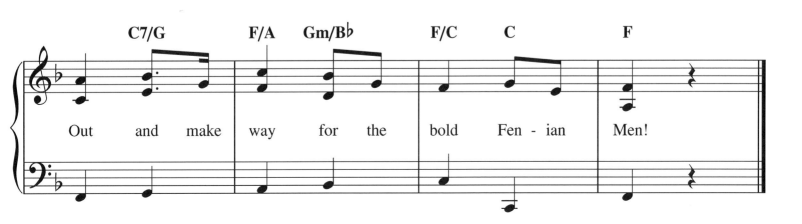

THE BARD OF ARMAGH

Traditional Irish Folk Song

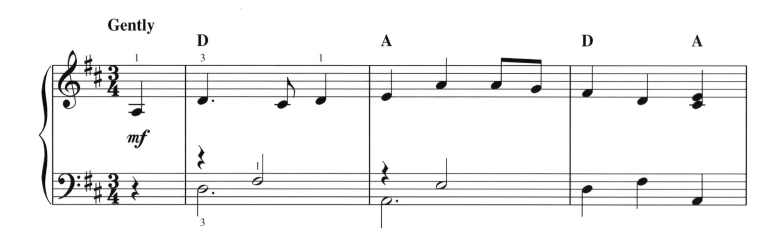

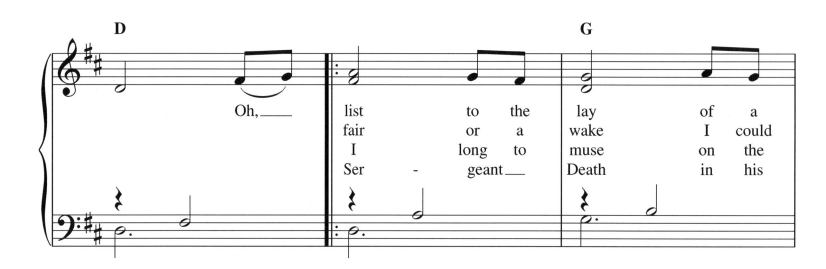

Oh,___
list to the lay of a
fair or a wake I could
I long to muse on the
Ser - geant___ Death in his

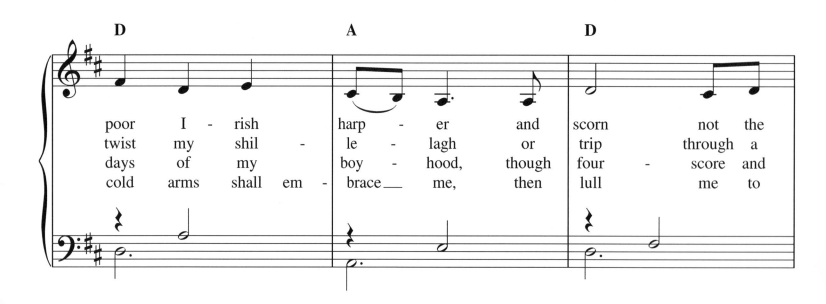

poor I - rish harp - er and scorn not the
twist my shil - le - lagh or trip through a
days of my boy - hood, though four - score and
cold arms shall em - brace___ me, then lull me to

BLACK VELVET BAND

Traditional Irish Folk Song

Waltz tempo

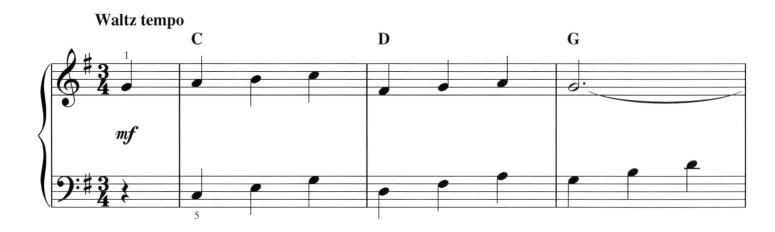

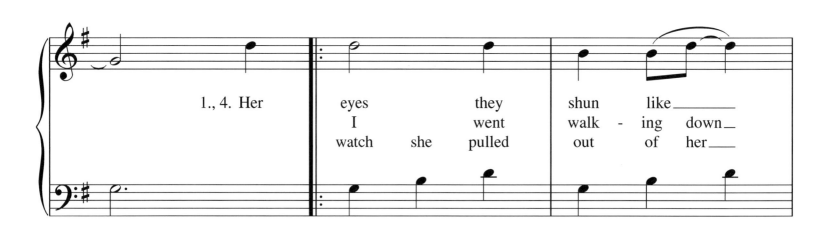

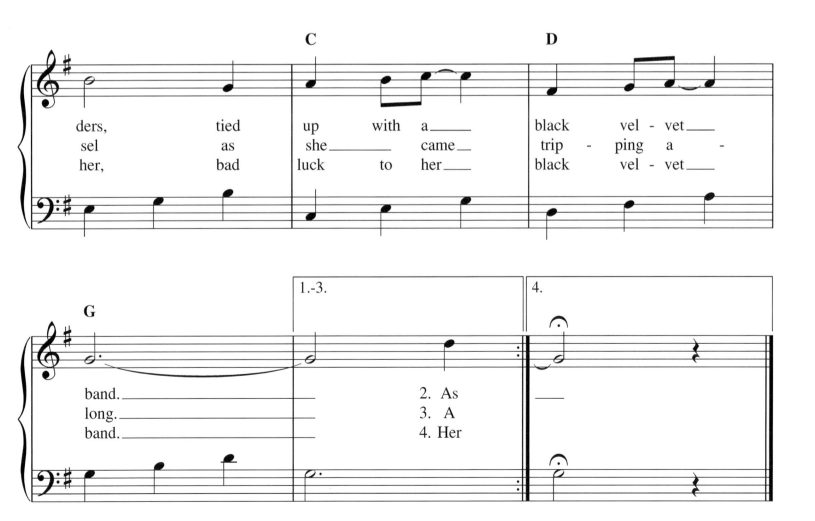

BOULAVOGUE

Irish Folk Song
Words and Music by P.J. McCALL

Moderately, in one

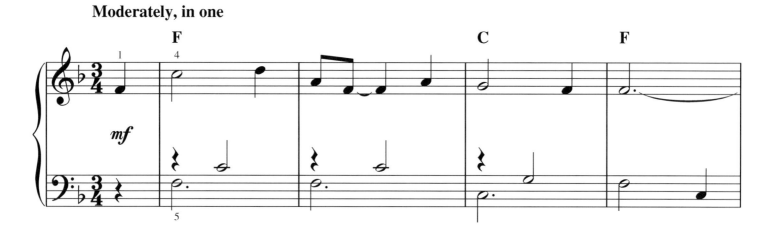

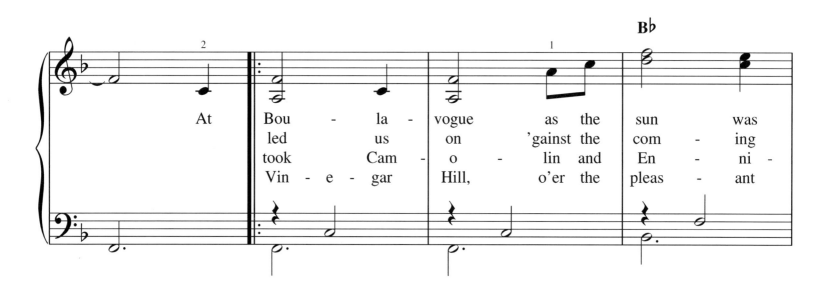

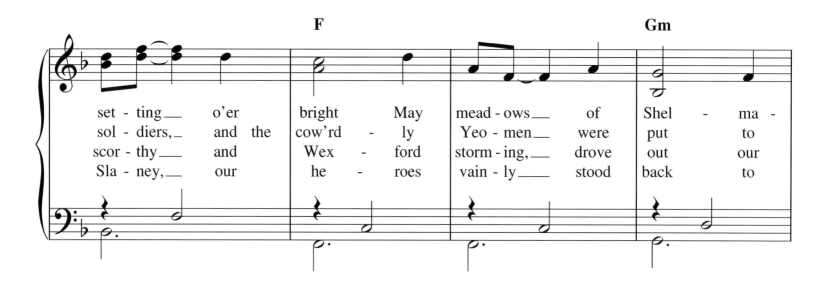

13

BRENNAN ON THE MOOR

Traditional

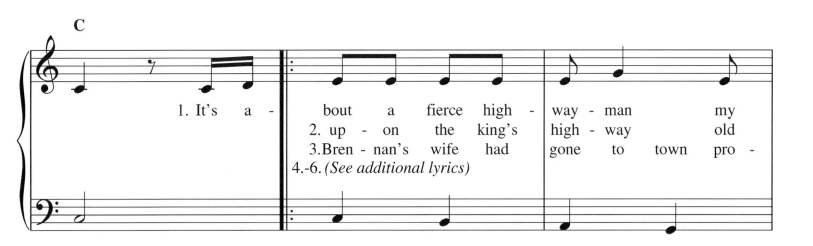

1. It's a-
2. up-
3.Bren-

bout a fierce high - way - man my
on the king's high - way old
nan's wife had gone to town pro -

4.-6.(See additional lyrics)

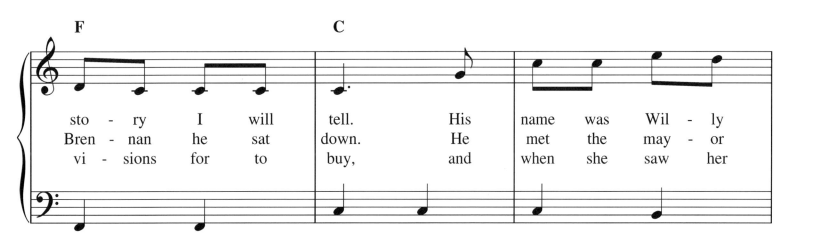

sto - ry I will tell. His name was Wil - ly
Bren - nan he will sat down. He met the may - or
vi - sions for to buy, and when she saw her

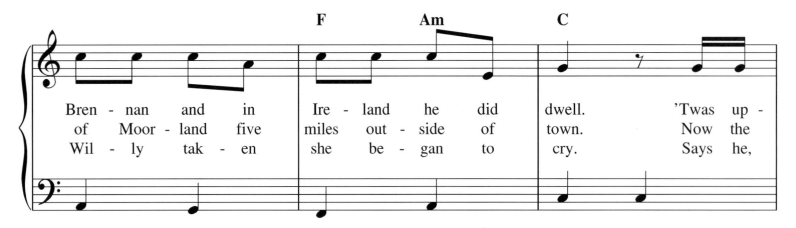

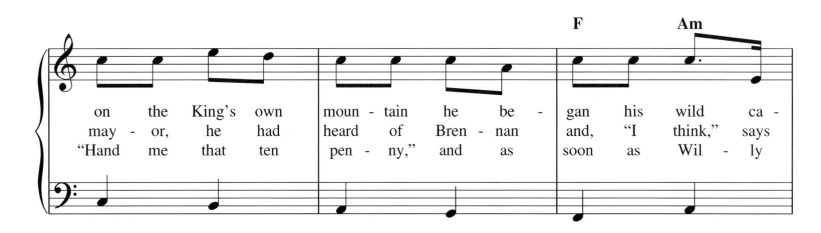

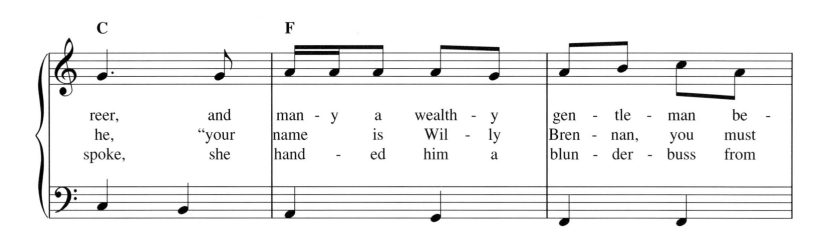

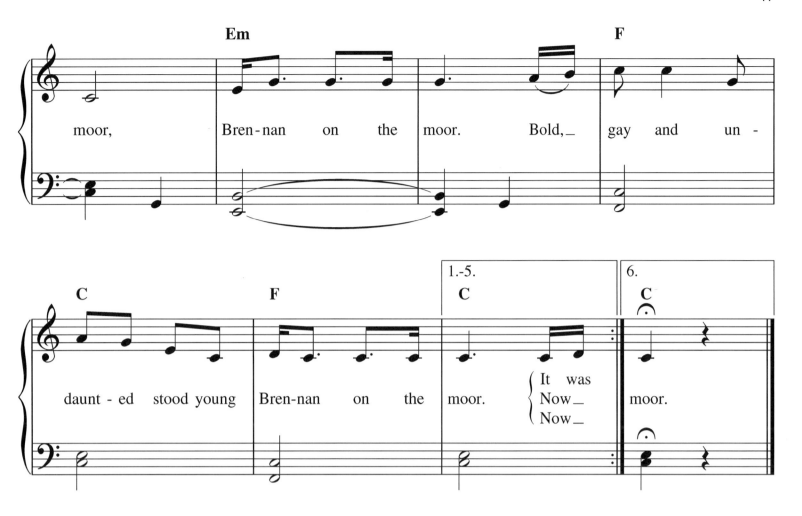

Additional Lyrics

4. Now Brennan got his blunderbuss, my story I'll unfold.
He caused the mayor to tremble and deliver up his gold.
Five thousand pounds were offered for his apprehension there,
But Brennan and the peddler to the mountain did repair.
Oh, it's Brennan on the moor, Brennan on the moor.
Bold, gay and undaunted stood young Brennan on the moor.

5. Now Brennan is an outlaw all on some mountain high.
With infantry and cavalry to take him they did try.
But he laughed at them and he scorned at them until, it was said,
By a false-hearted woman he was cruelly betrayed.
Oh, it's Brennan on the moor, Brennan on the moor.
Bold, gay and undaunted stood young Brennan on the moor.

6. They hung him at the crossroads; in chains he swung and died.
But still they say that in the night some do see him ride.
They see him with his blunderbuss in the midnight chill;
Along, along the king's highway rides Willy Brennan still.
Oh, it's Brennan on the moor, Brennan on the moor.
Bold, gay and undaunted stood young Brennan on the moor.

BUTCHER BOY

Traditional Irish Folk Song

Moderately

1. In Lon-don

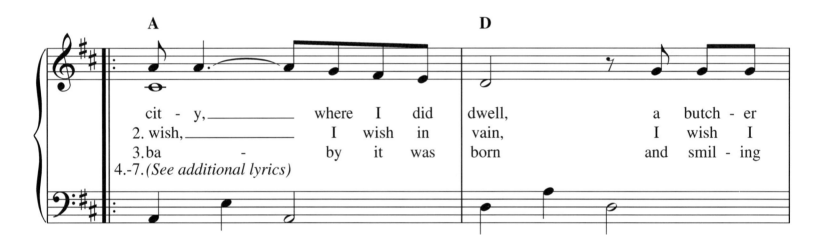

cit - y,_____ where I did dwell, a butch - er
2. wish,_____ I wish in vain, I wish I
3. ba - by it was born and smil - ing
4.-7.*(See additional lyrics)*

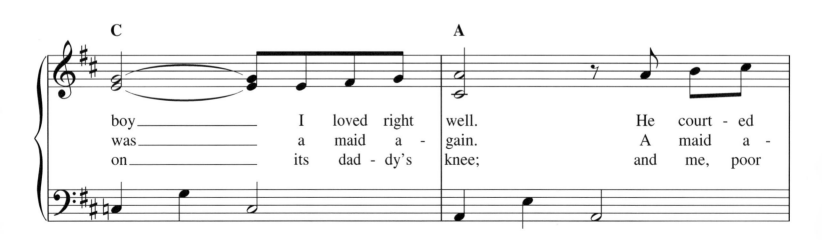

boy_____ I loved right well. He court - ed
was_____ a maid a - gain. A maid a -
on_____ its dad - dy's knee; and me, poor

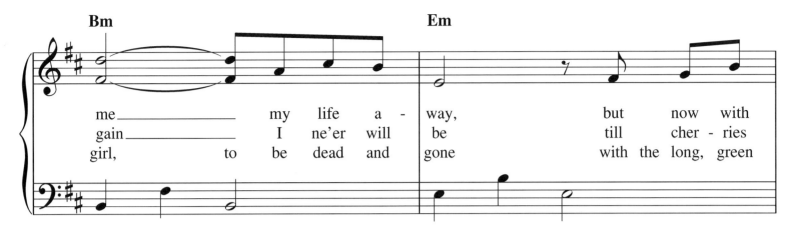

Additional Lyrics

4. She went upstairs to go to bed,
And calling to her mother said,
"Give me a chair till I sit down
And a pen and ink till I write down."

5. At ev'ry word she dropped a tear,
At ev'ry line cried, "Willie, dear,
Oh, what a foolish girl was I
To be led astray by a butcher boy."

6. He went upstairs and the door he broke;
He found her hanging from a rope.
He took his knife and he cut her down,
And in her pocket these words he found:

7. "Oh, make my grave large, wide and deep;
Put a marble stone at my head and feet.
And in the middle a turtledove,
That the world may know that I died for love."

CARRICKFERGUS

Traditional Irish Folk Song

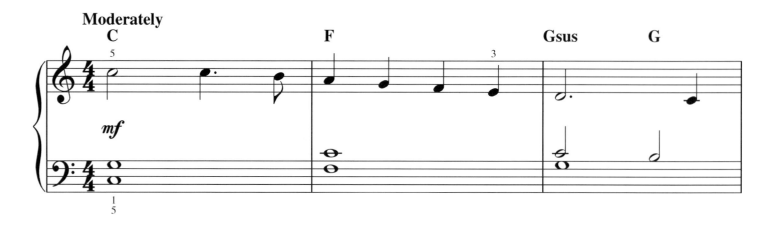

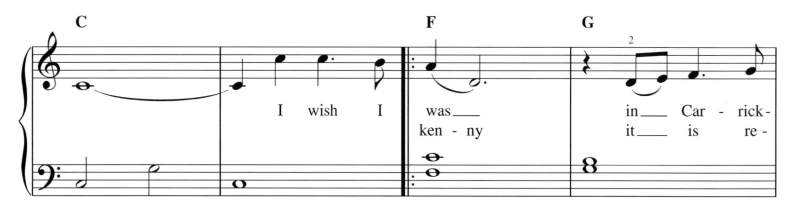

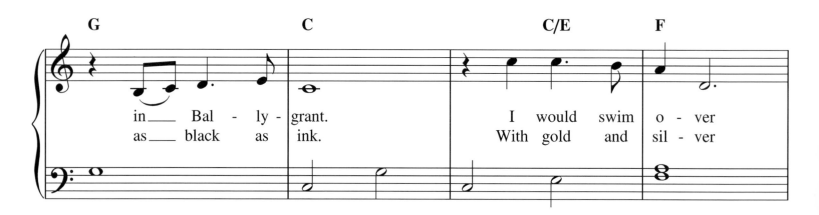

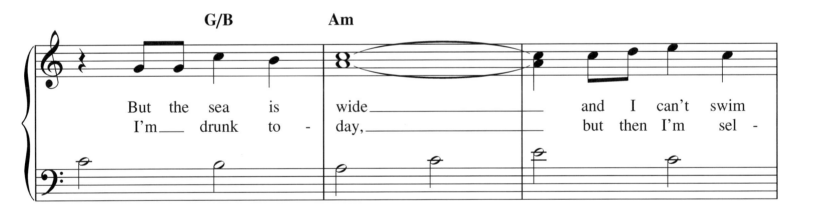

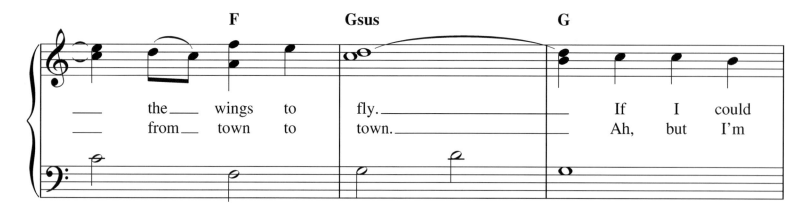

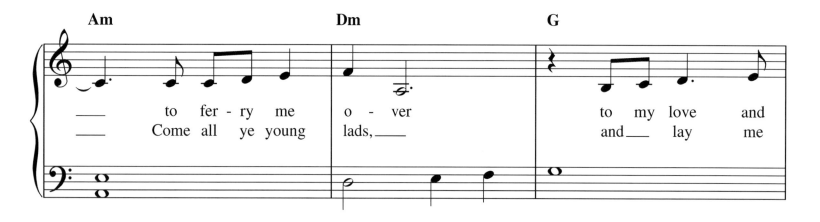

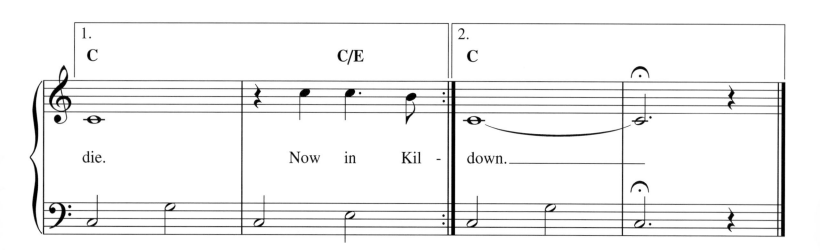

COME BACK TO ERIN

Irish Folk Song

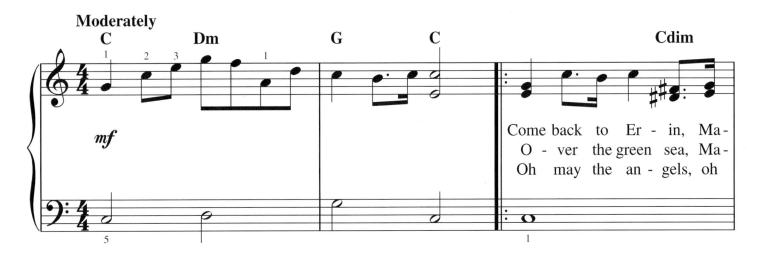

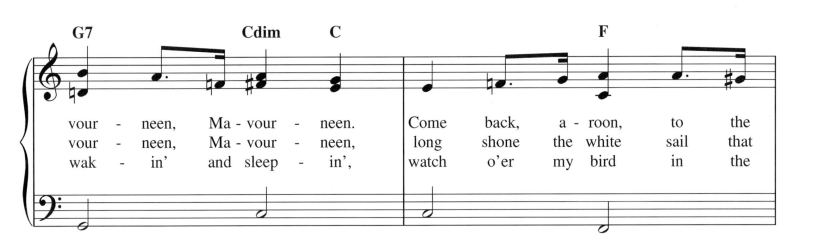

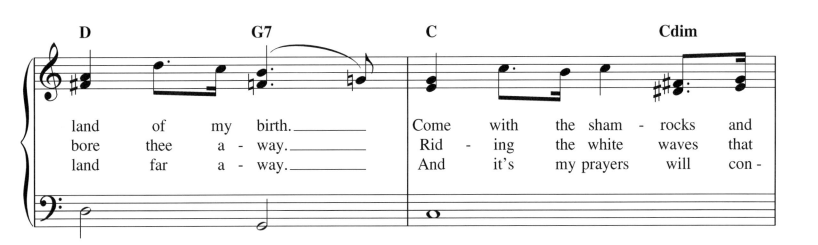

24

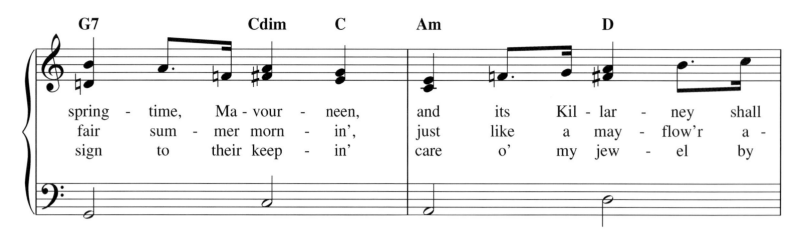

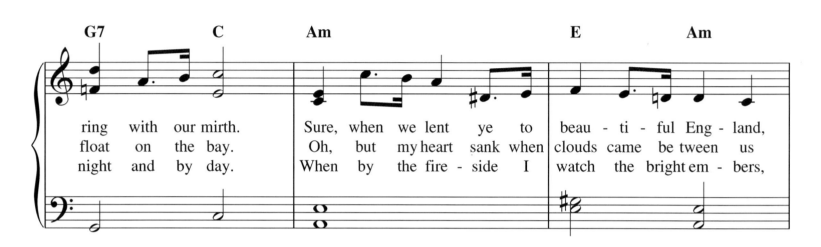

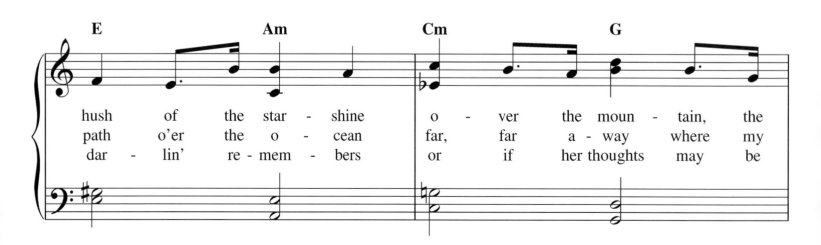

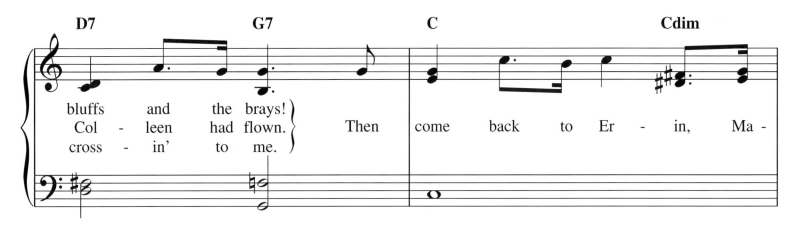

bluffs and the brays!
Col - leen had flown.
cross - in' to me.

Then come back to Er - in, Ma -

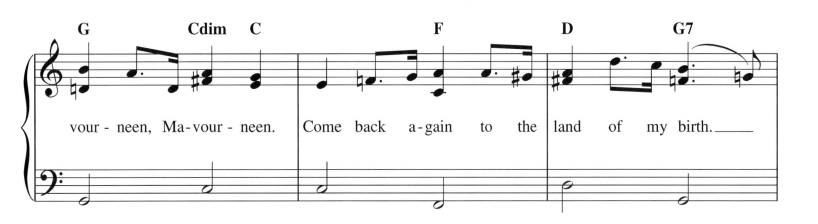

vour - neen, Ma - vour - neen. Come back a - gain to the land of my birth.____

Come back to Er - in, Ma - vour - neen, Ma - vour - neen. And__ its Kil - lar - ney shall

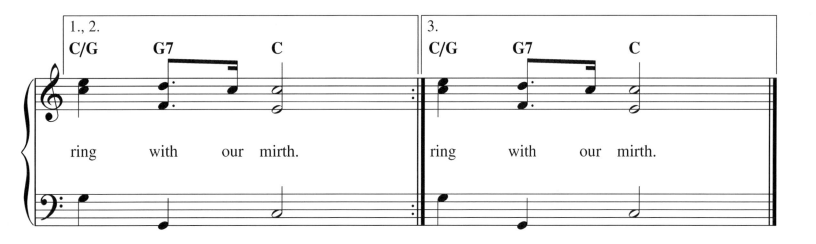

1., 2.

ring with our mirth.

3.

ring with our mirth.

CLIFFS OF DONEEN

Traditional Irish Folk Song

Moderately

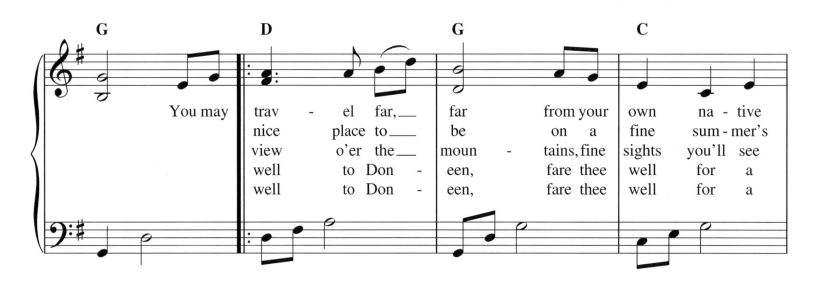

You may | trav - el far,___ | far | from your | own | na - tive
nice | place to___ | be | on a | fine | sum - mer's
view | o'er the___ | moun - tains, fine | sights | you'll | see
well | to Don - | een, | fare thee | well | for a
well | to Don - | een, | fare thee | well | for a

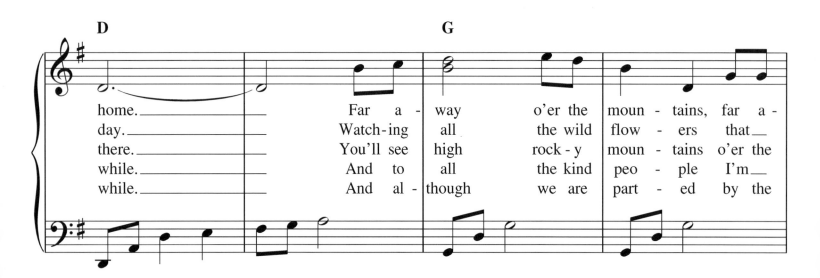

home.___ | | Far a - way | o'er the | moun - tains, far a -
day.___ | | Watch-ing all | the wild | flow - ers that___
there.___ | | You'll see high | rock - y | moun - tains o'er the
while.___ | | And to all | the kind | peo - ple I'm___
while.___ | | And al - though | we are | part - ed by the

THE CROPPY BOY

Eighteenth Century Irish Folk Song

Moderately

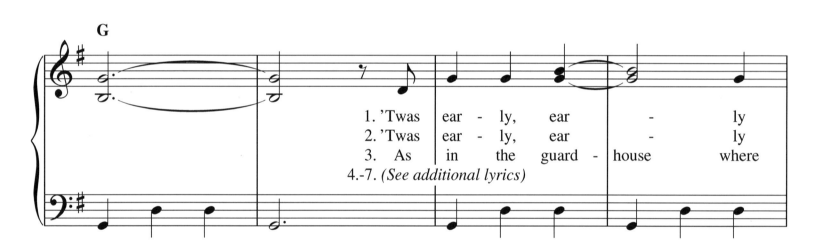

1. 'Twas ear - ly, ear - ly
2. 'Twas ear - ly, ear - ly
3. As in the guard - house where
4.-7. *(See additional lyrics)*

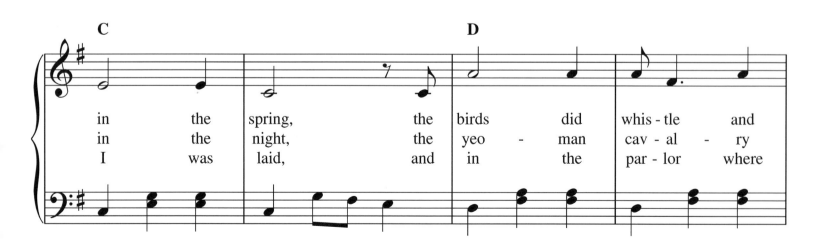

in the spring, the birds did whis - tle and
in the night, the yeo - man cav - al - ry
I was laid, and in the par - lor where

Additional Lyrics

4. As I was passing my father's door, my brother William stood at the door.
   My aged father stood there also, my tender mother her hair she tore.

5. As I was going up Wexford Hill, who could blame me to cry my fill?
   I looked behind and I looked before, my aged mother I shall see no more.

6. As I was mounted on the scaffold high, my aged father was standing by.
   My aged father did me deny, and the name he gave me was the croppy boy.

7. 'Twas in the Dungannon this young man died, and in Dungannon his body lies.
   And you good people that do pass by, oh, shed a tear for the croppy boy.

DOWN BY THE SALLEY GARDENS

Traditional Irish Folk Song

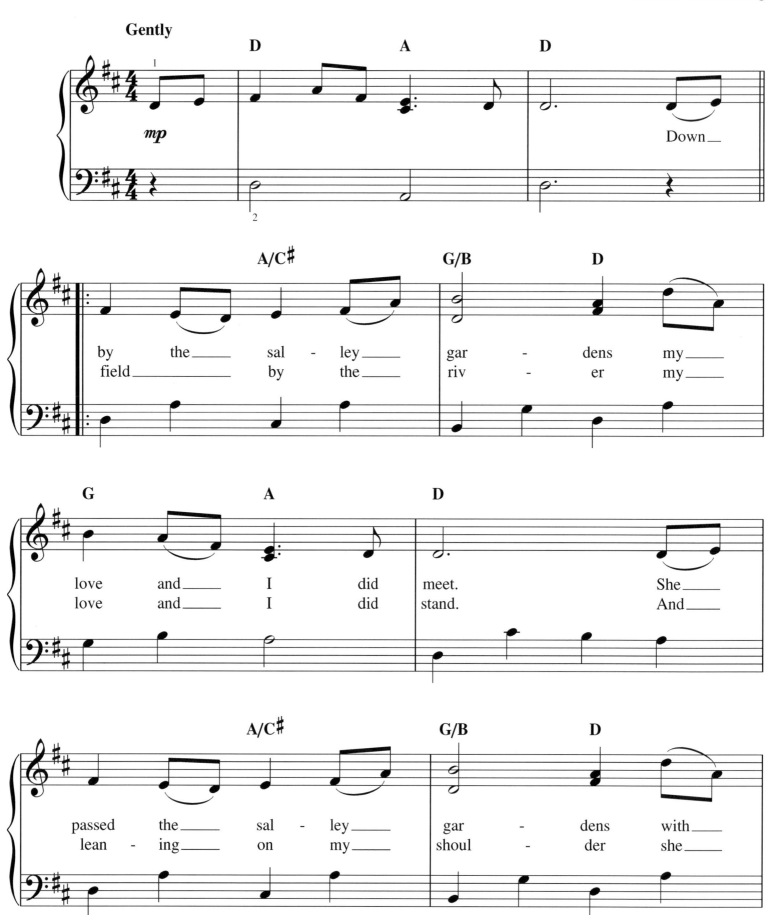

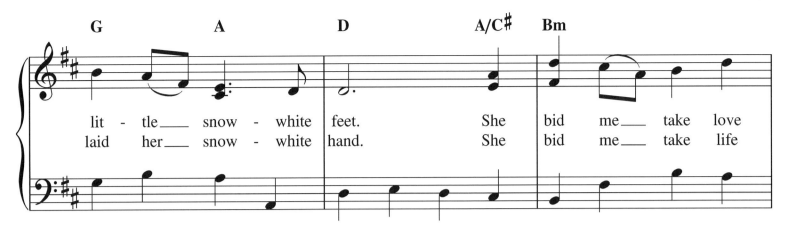

lit - tle___ snow - white feet. She bid me___ take love
laid her___ snow - white hand. She bid me___ take life

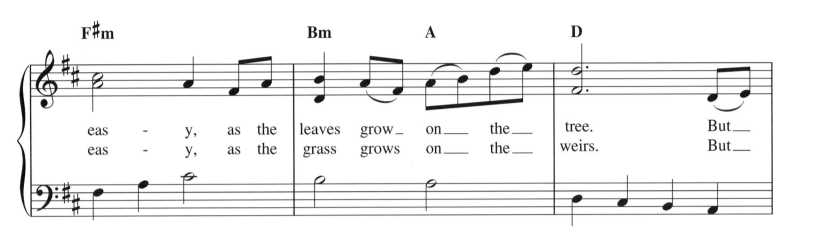

eas - y, as the leaves grow___ on___ the___ tree. But___
eas - y, as the grass grows on___ the___ weirs. But___

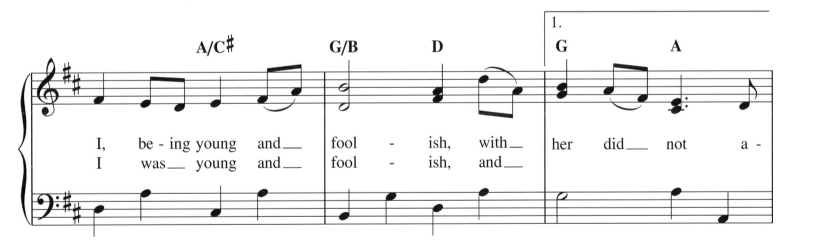

I, be - ing young and___ fool - ish, with___ her did___ not a-
I was___ young and___ fool - ish, and___

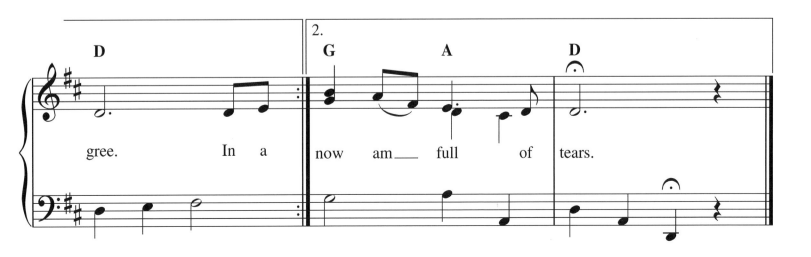

gree. In a
now am___ full of tears.

FINNEGAN'S WAKE

Traditional Irish Folk Song

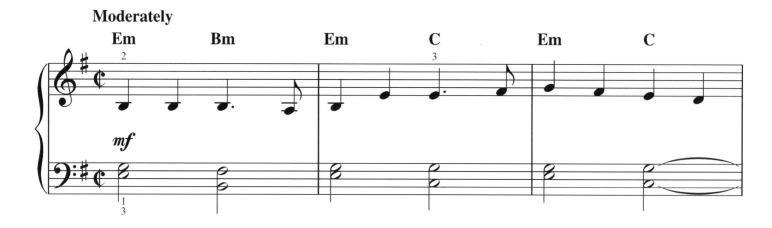

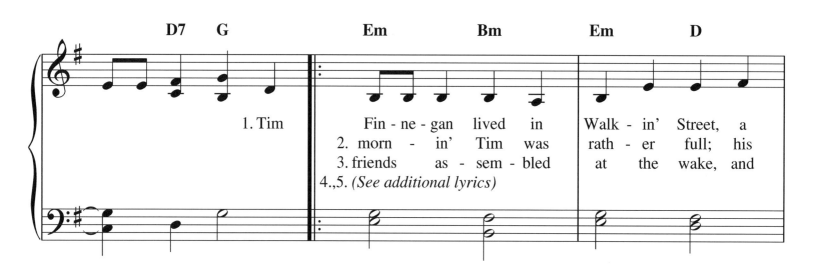

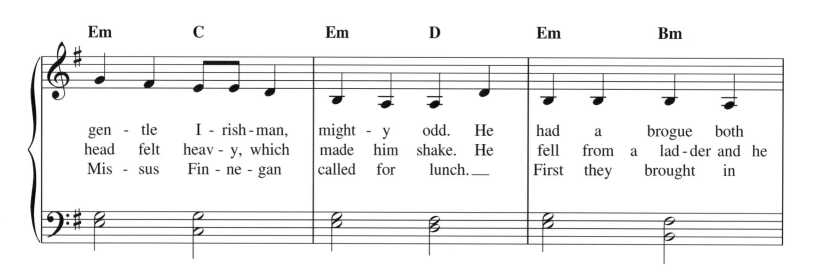

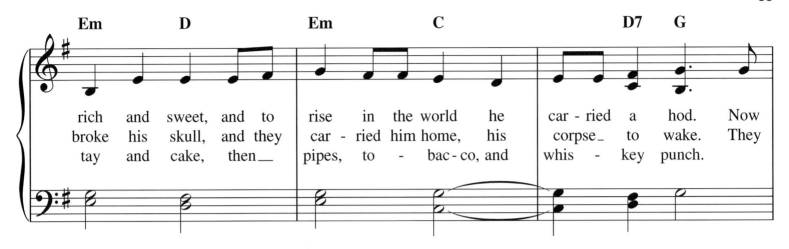

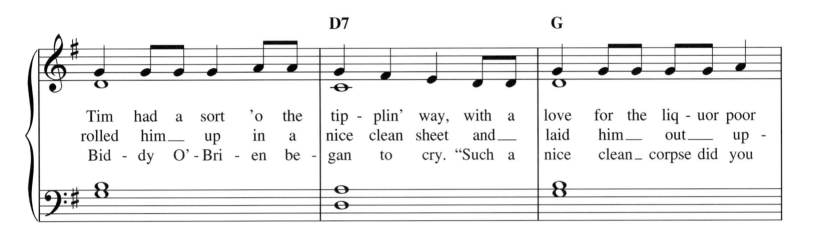

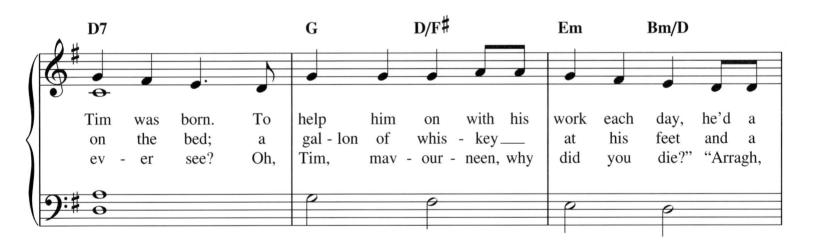

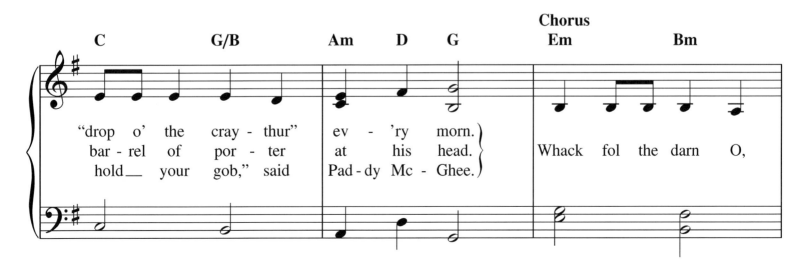

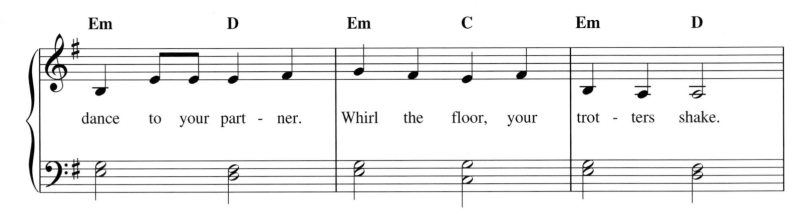

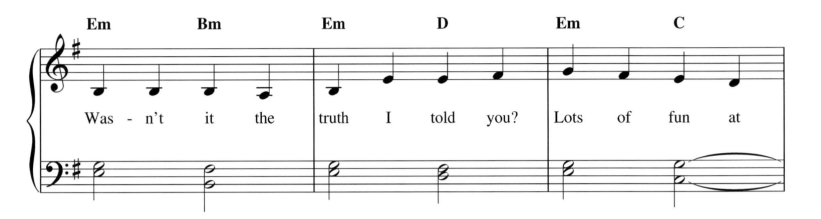

Additional Lyrics

4. Then Maggie O'Connor took up the job.
   "Oh Biddy," says she, "you're wrong, I'm sure."
   Biddy, she gave her a belt in the gob
   And left her sprawlin' on the floor.
   And then the war did soon engage,
   'Twas woman to woman and man to man.
   Shillelaigh law was all the rage,
   And a row and ruction soon began.
   Chorus

5. Then Mickey Maloney ducked his head
   When a noggin of whiskey flew at him.
   It missed, and falling on the bed,
   The liquor scattered over Tim!
   The corpse revives; see how he rises!
   Timothy, rising from the bed,
   Said, "Whirl your whiskey around like blazes,
   Thanum an Dhul! Do you think I'm dead?"
   Chorus

LEAVING OF LIVERPOOL

Irish Sea Chantey

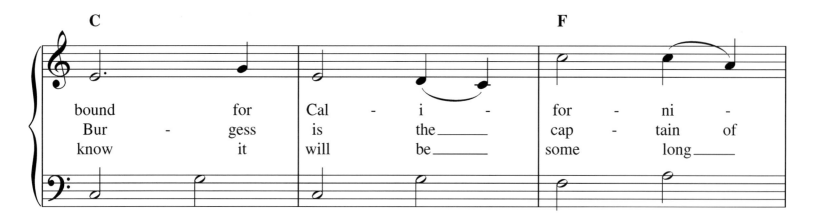

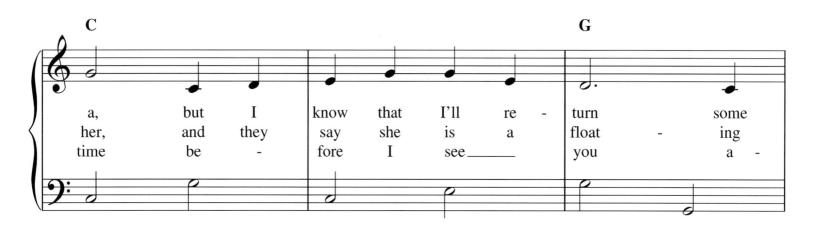

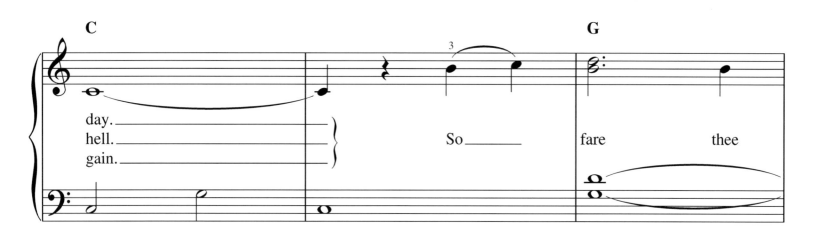

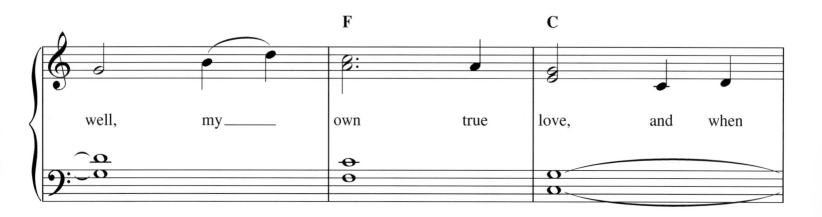

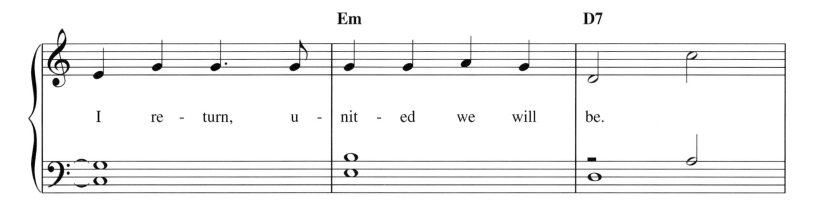

I re - turn, u - nit - ed we will be.

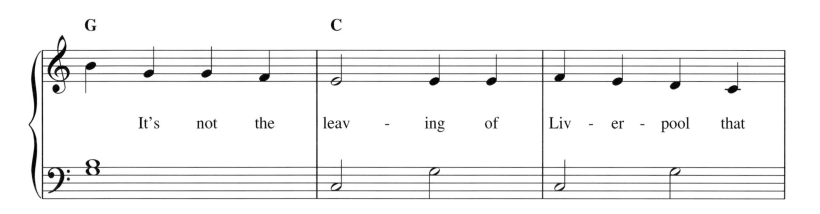

It's not the leav - ing of Liv - er - pool that

grieves_____ me, but, my dar - ling, when I

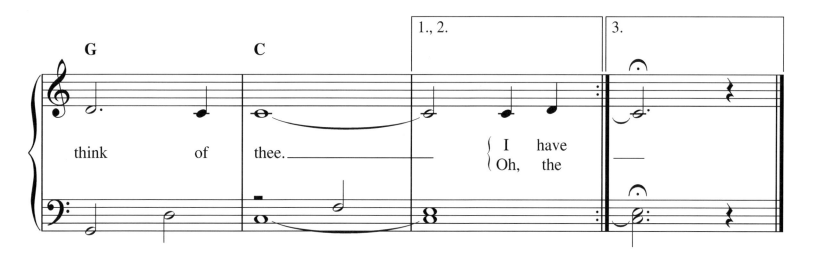

think of thee._____ I have / Oh, the

THE FOGGY DEW

Traditional Irish Folk Song

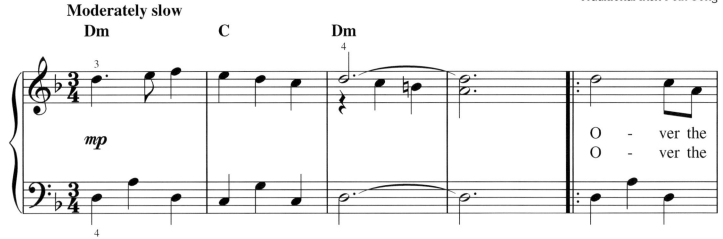

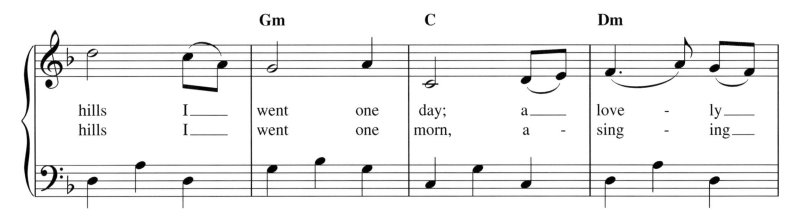

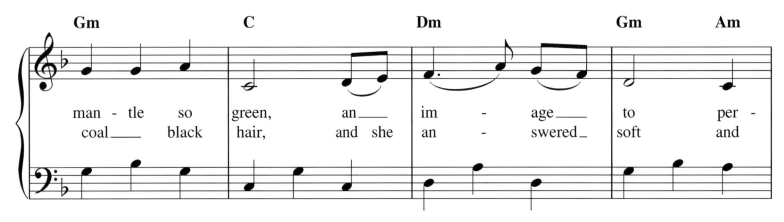

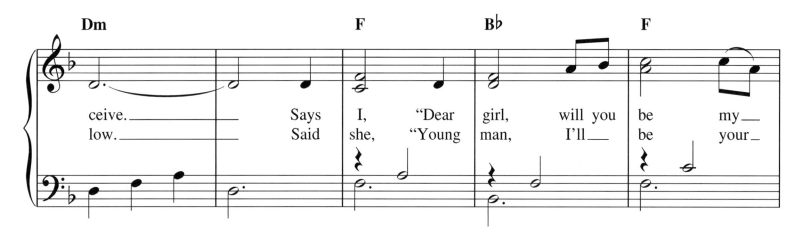

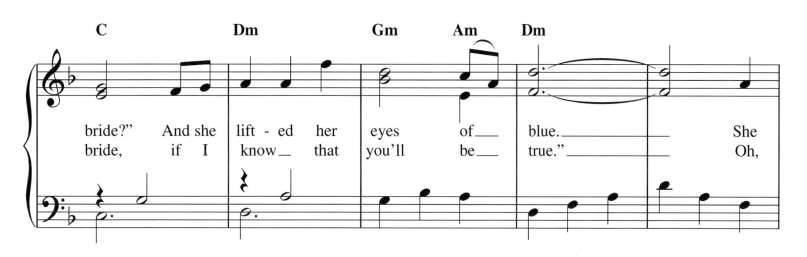

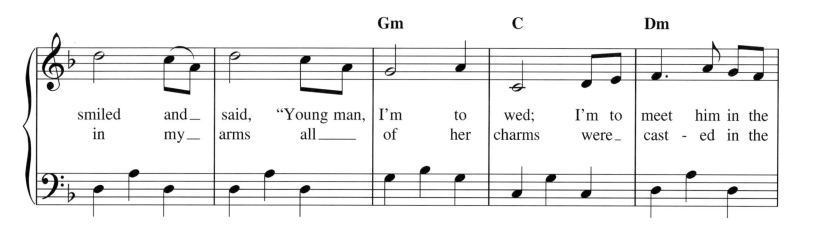

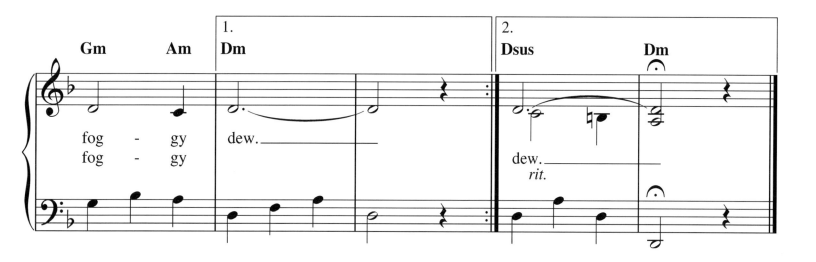

GREEN GROW THE RASHES, O

Traditional Irish Folk Song

1. There's

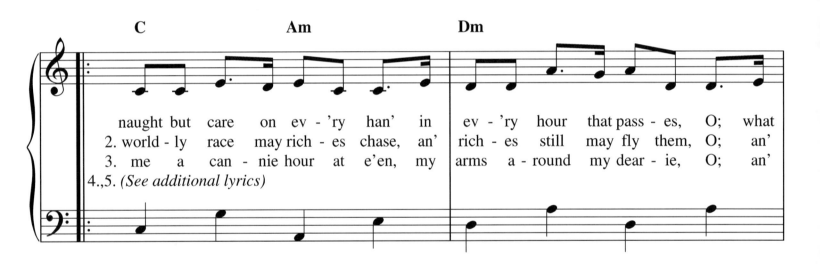

naught but care on ev-'ry han' in ev-'ry hour that pass-es, O; what
2. world-ly race may rich-es chase, an' rich-es still may fly them, O; an'
3. me a can-nie hour at e'en, my arms a-round my dear-ie, O; an'

4.,5. *(See additional lyrics)*

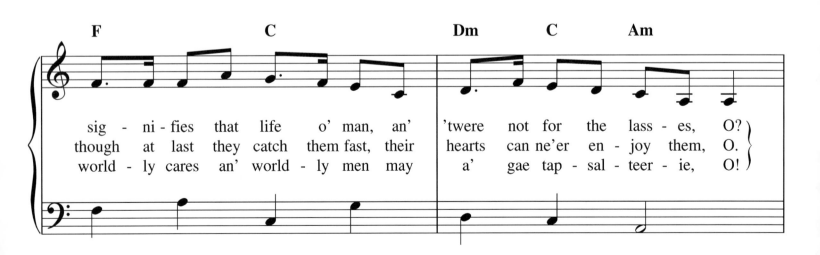

sig-ni-fies that life o' man, an' 'twere not for the lass-es, O?
though at last they catch them fast, their hearts can ne'er en-joy them, O.
world-ly cares an' world-ly men may a' gae tap-sal-teer-ie, O!

Chorus

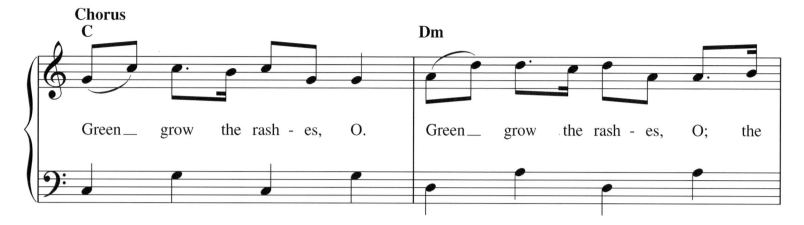

Green — grow the rash - es, O. Green — grow the rash - es, O; the

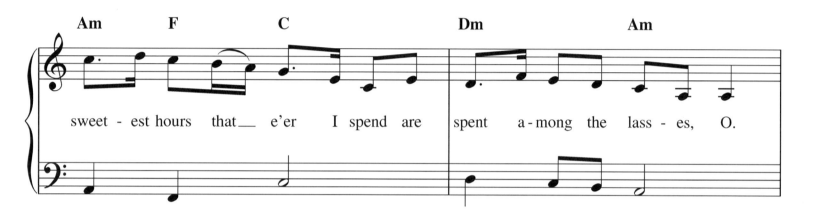

sweet - est hours that — e'er I spend are spent a - mong the lass - es, O.

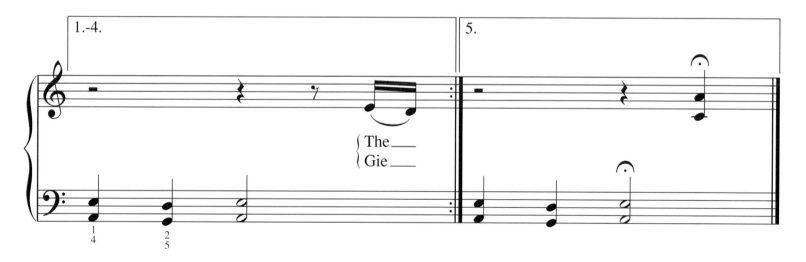

1.-4.

{ The —
{ Gie —

5.

Additional Lyrics

4. An' you sae douce, ye sneer at this,
   Ye're naught but senseless asses, O;
   The wisest man the world e'er saw,
   He dearly loved the lasses, O.
   Chorus

5. Auld nature swears the lovely dears
   Her noblest work she classes, O;
   Her 'prentice han' she tried on man,
   An' then she made the lasses, O.
   Chorus

I KNOW MY LOVE

Traditional Irish Folk Song

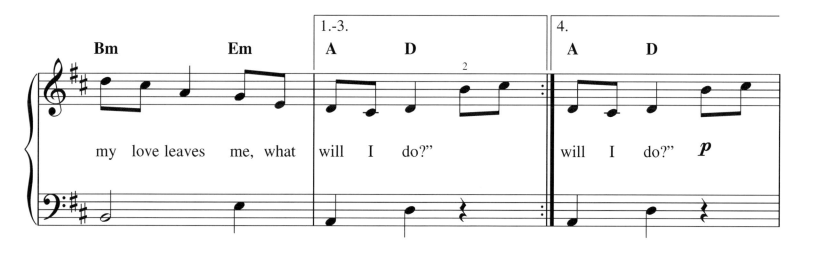

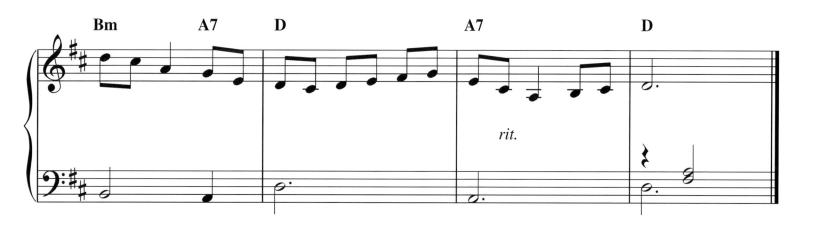

I'LL TELL ME MA

Traditional Irish Folk Song

Moderately fast

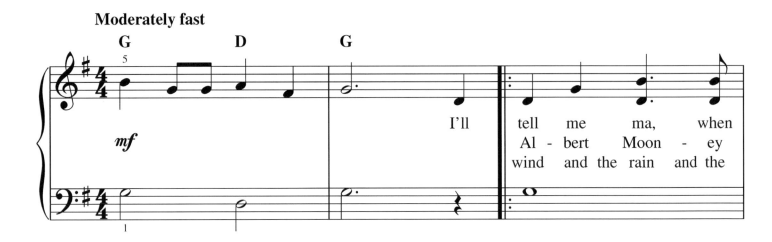

I'll tell me ma, when
Al - bert Moon - ey
wind and the rain and the

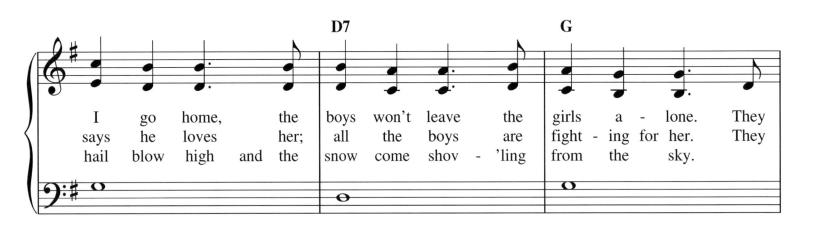

I go home, the boys won't leave the girls a - lone. They
says he loves her; all the boys are fight - ing for her. They
hail blow high and the snow come shov - 'ling from the sky.

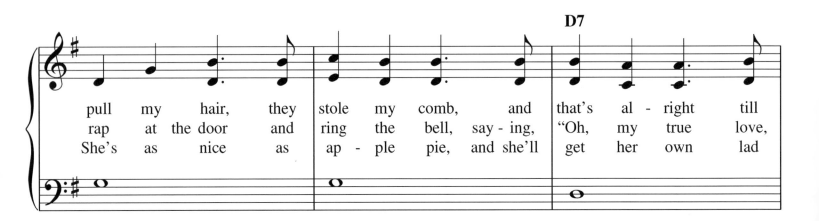

pull my hair, they stole my comb, and that's al - right till
rap at the door and ring the bell, say - ing, "Oh, my true love,
She's as nice as ap - ple pie, and she'll get her own lad

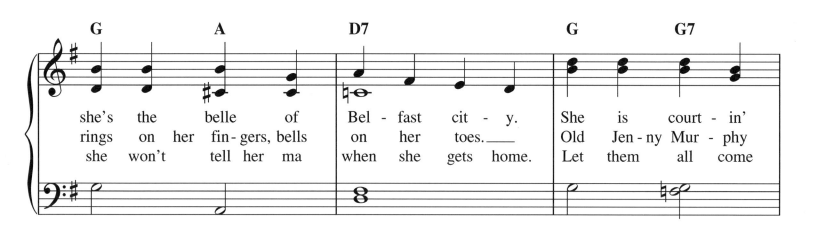

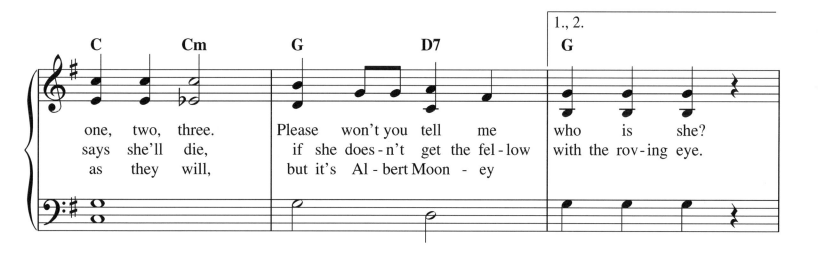

THE IRISH ROVER

Traditional Irish Folk Song

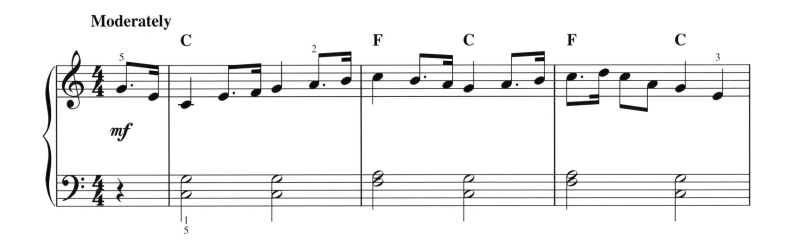

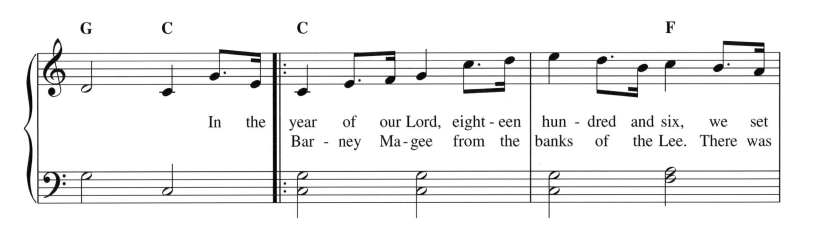

In the year of our Lord, eight-een hun-dred and six, we set
Bar-ney Ma-gee from the banks of the Lee. There was

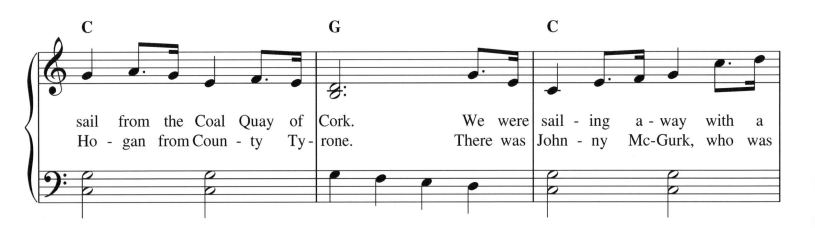

sail from the Coal Quay of Cork. We were sail-ing a-way with a
Ho-gan from Coun-ty Ty-rone. There was John-ny Mc-Gurk, who was

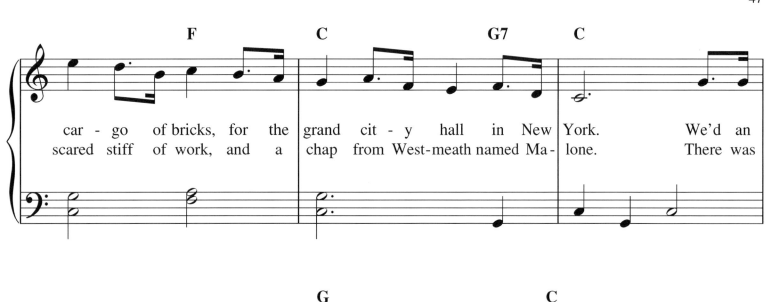

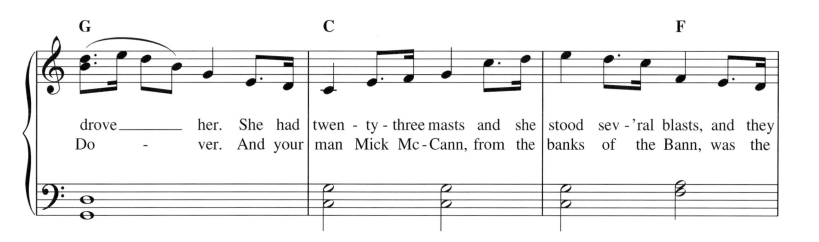

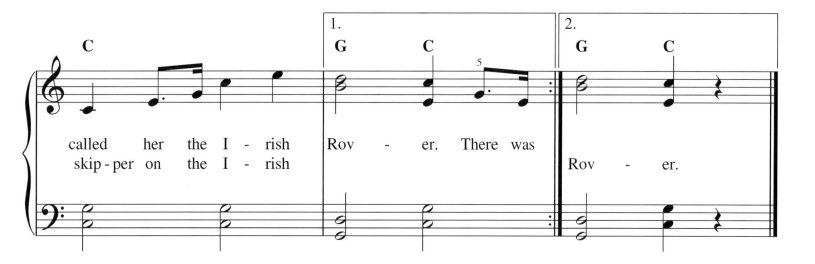

JUG OF PUNCH

Ulster Folk Song

THE LARK IN THE CLEAR AIR

Words and Music by
SIR SAMUEL FERGUSON

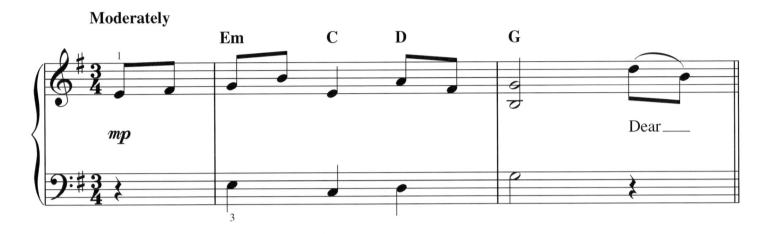

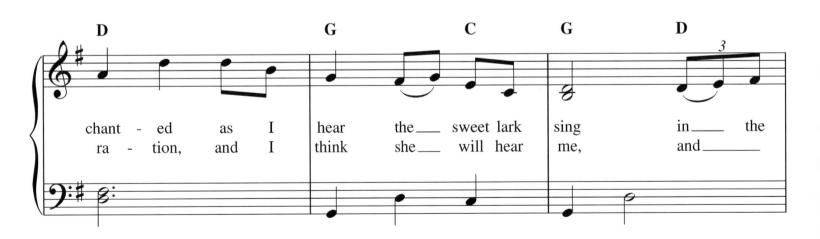

clear___ air of the day. For a ten - der, beam - ing___
will___ not say me nay. It is this that gives___ my___

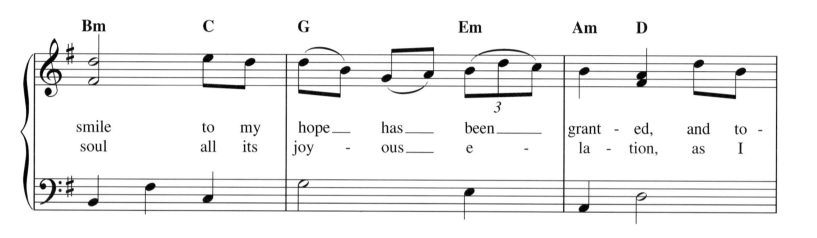

smile to my hope___ has___ been_____ grant - ed, and to -
soul all its joy - ous___ e - la - tion, as I

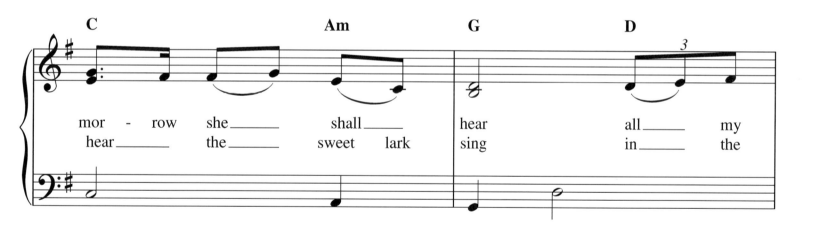

mor - row she_____ shall_____ hear all_____ my
hear_____ the_____ sweet lark sing in_____ the

fond___ heart would___ say. I shall
clear___ air of the day.

THE MEETING OF THE WATERS

Traditional Irish Folk Song

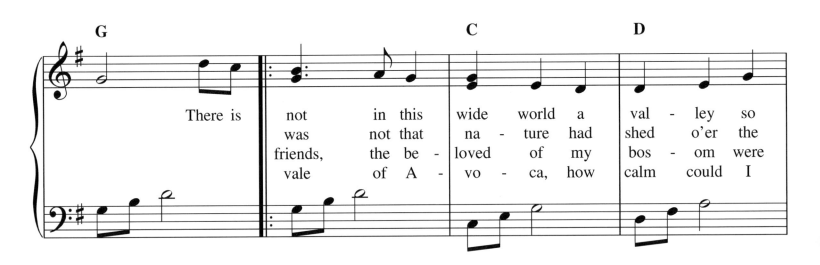

There is | not | in this | wide world a | val - ley so
was | not that | na - ture had | shed o'er the
friends, the be - | loved of my | bos - om were
vale of A - | vo - ca, how | calm could I

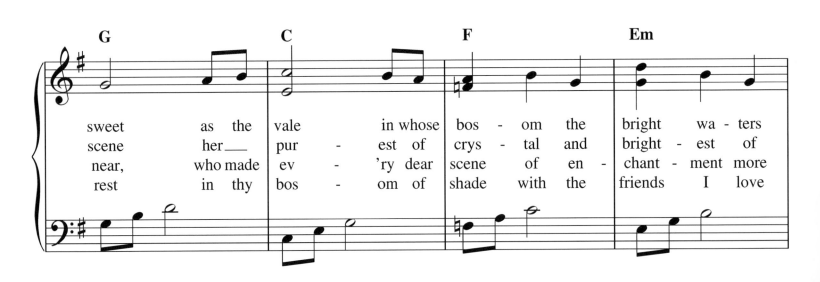

sweet | as the | vale | in whose | bos - om the | bright wa - ters
scene her | pur - est of | crys - tal and | bright - est of
near, who made | ev - 'ry dear | scene of en - | chant - ment more
rest in thy | bos - om of | shade with the | friends I love

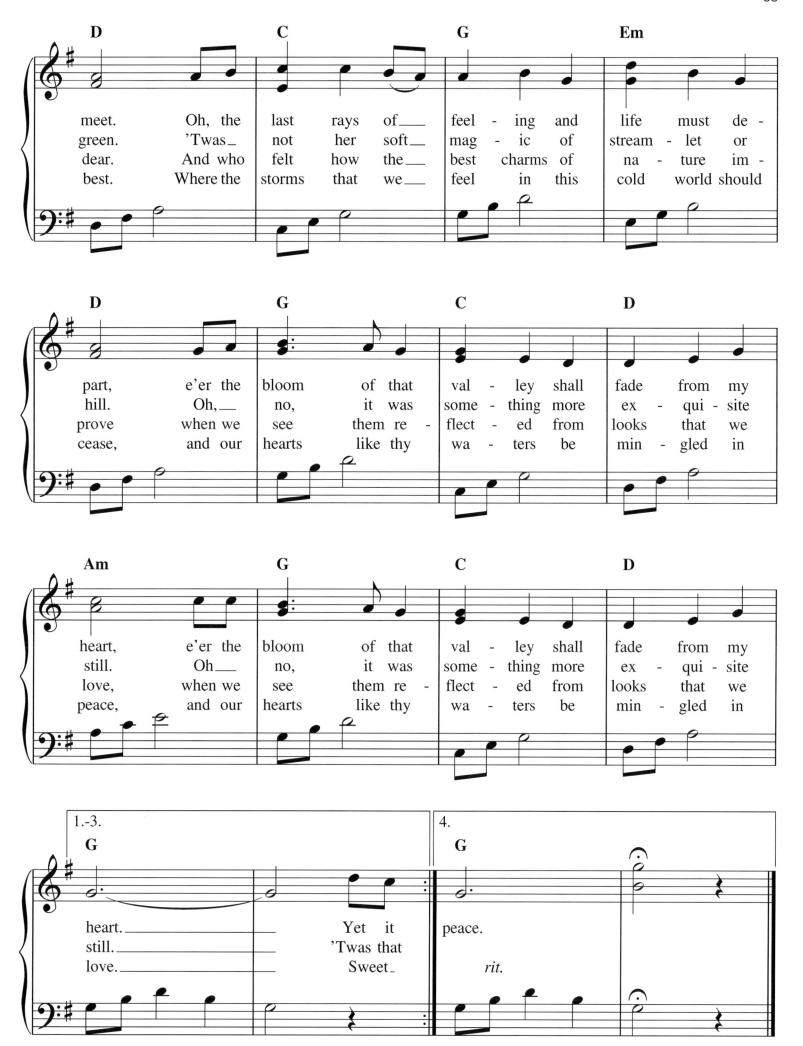

THE MOUNTAINS OF MOURNE

Words by PERCY FRENCH
Traditional Irish Melody

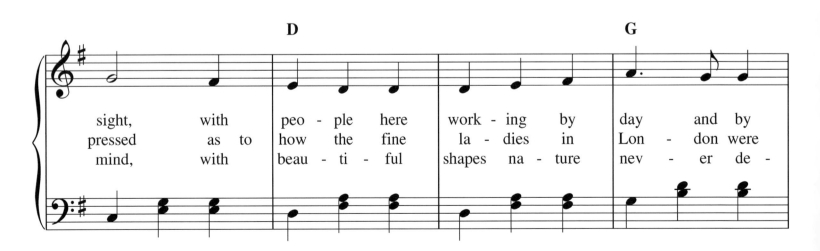

Oh,

Mar - y, this
lieve that when
beau - ti - ful

Lon - don's a
writ - ing a
girls here, oh

won - der - ful
wish you ex -
nev - er you

sight, with
pressed as to
mind, with

peo - ple here
how the fine
beau - ti - ful

work - ing by
la - dies in
shapes na - ture

day and by
Lon - don were
nev - er de -

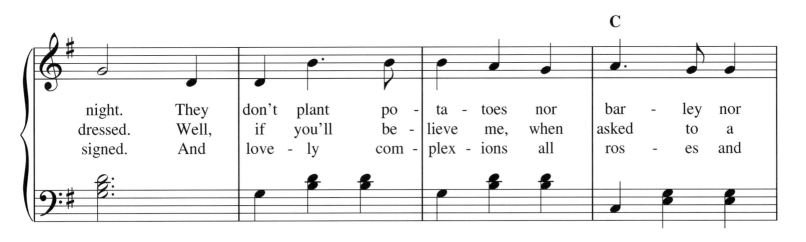

C

night. They / dressed. Well, / signed. And

don't plant po - ta - toes nor / if you'll be - lieve me, when / love - ly com - plex - ions all

bar - ley nor / asked to a / ros - es and

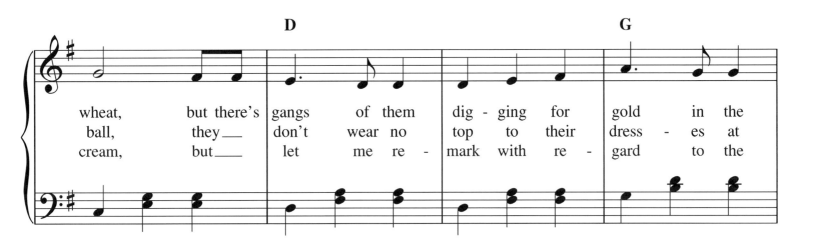

D   **G**

wheat, but there's / ball, they __ / cream, but __

gangs of them / don't wear no / let me re -

dig - ging for / top to their / mark with re -

gold in the / dress - es at / gard to the

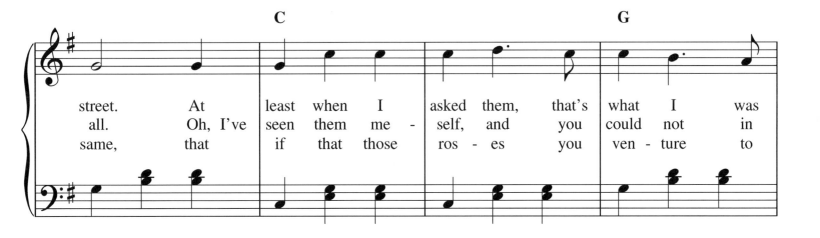

C   **G**

street. At / all. Oh, I've / same, that

least when I / seen them me - / if that those

asked them, that's / self, and you / ros - es you

what I was / could not in / ven - ture to

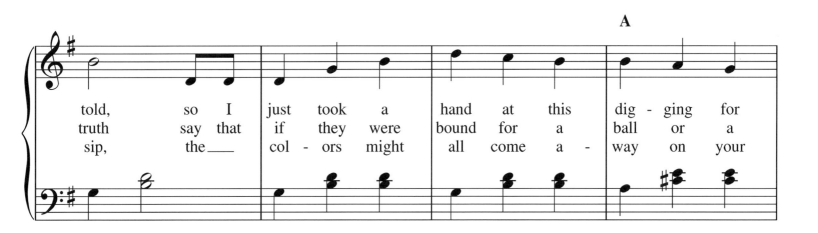

A

told, so I / truth say that / sip, the __

just took a / if they were / col - ors might

hand at this / bound for a / all come a -

dig - ging for / ball or a / way on your

gold. But for
bath. Don't be
lip. So I'll

all that I've
start - ing them
wait for the

found there, I
fash - ions, now,
wild rose that's

might as well
Mar - y Mc -
wait - ing for

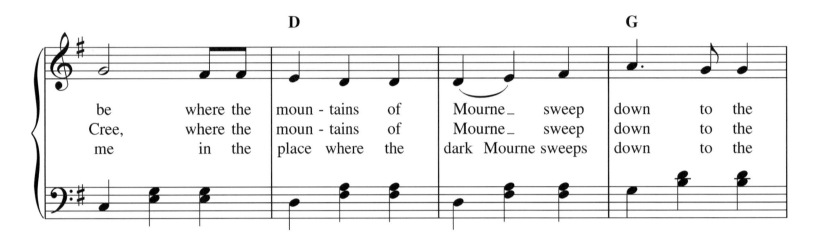

be where the
Cree, where the
me in the

moun - tains of
moun - tains of
place where the

Mourne sweep
Mourne sweep
dark Mourne sweeps

down to the
down to the
down to the

1., 2.

sea.
sea.
sea.

I be -
There's

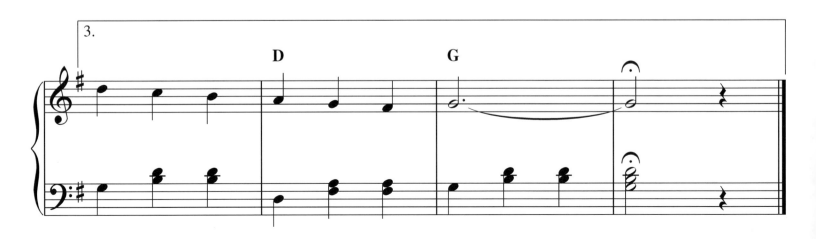

3.

A NATION ONCE AGAIN

Words and Music by
THOMAS DAVIS

When boy - hood's fire was
from that time, through
whis - pered, too, that
as I grew from

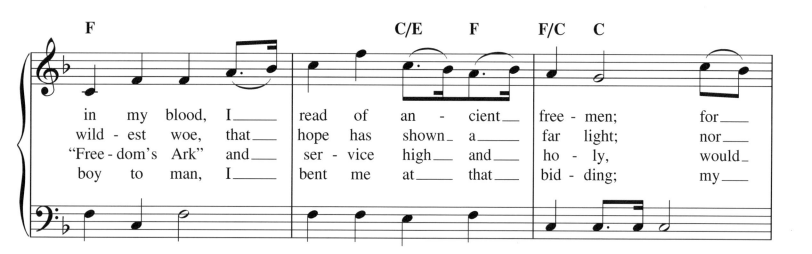

in my blood, I read of an - cient free - men; for
wild - est woe, that hope has shown a far light; nor
"Free - dom's Ark" and ser - vice high and ho - ly, would
boy to man, I bent me at that bid - ding; my

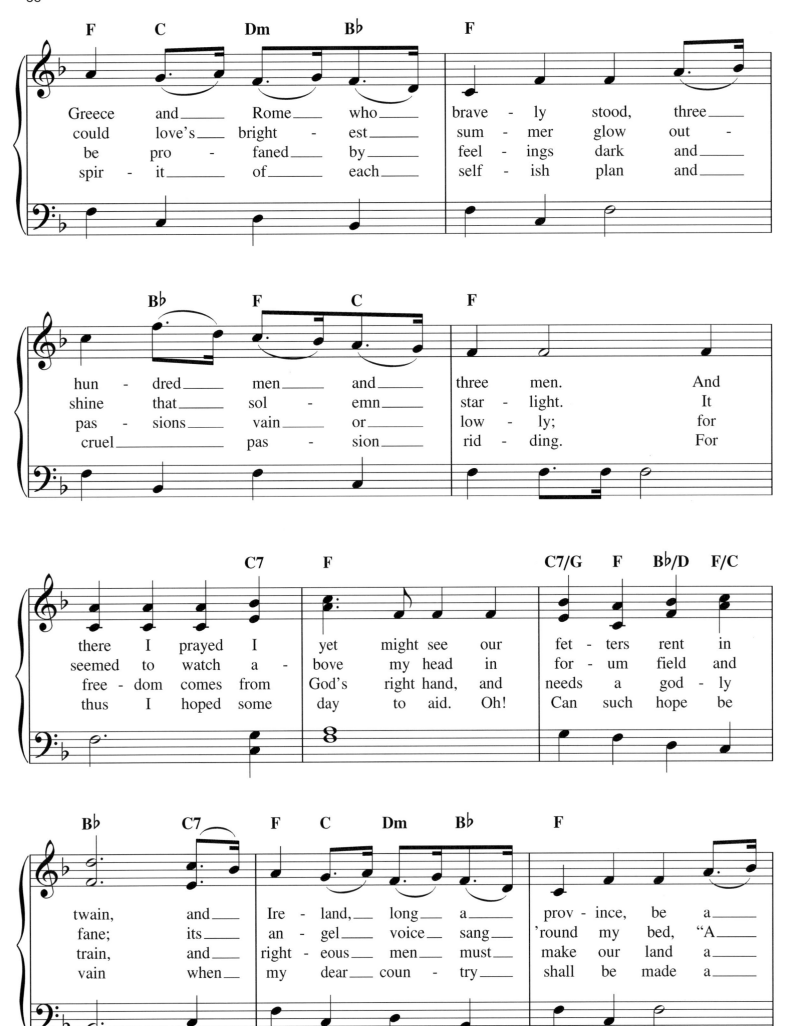

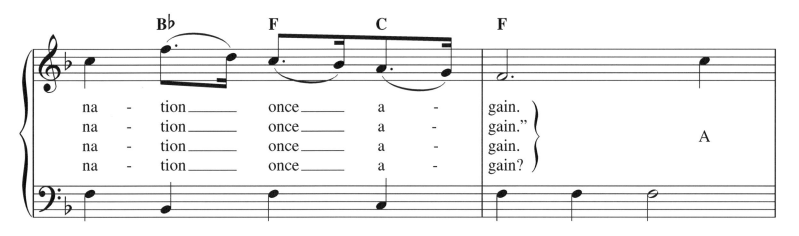

na - tion_____ once_____ a - gain.
na - tion_____ once_____ a - gain."
na - tion_____ once_____ a - gain.
na - tion_____ once_____ a - gain?

A

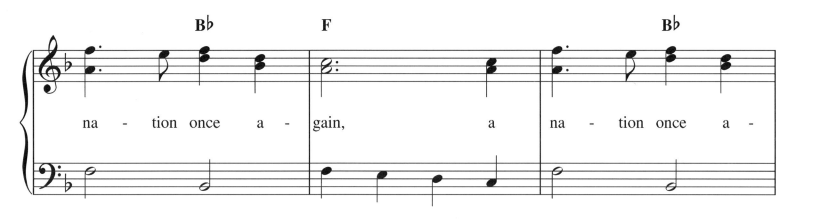

na - tion once a - gain,   a na - tion once a -

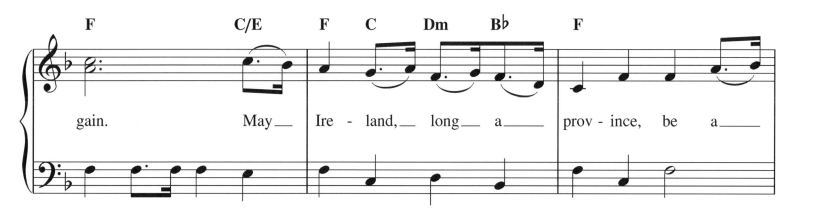

gain.   May__ Ire - land,__ long__ a__ prov - ince, be a__

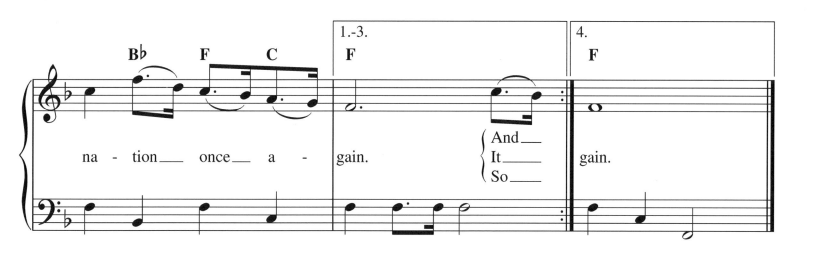

na - tion__ once__ a - gain.

And__
It____
So__

gain.

PADDY WORKS ON THE RAILWAY

Traditional

Additional Lyrics

4. In eighteen hundred and forty-four, I landed on Columbia's shore.
   I landed on Columbia's shore, to work upon the railway.
   Chorus

5. In eighteen hundred and forty-five, when Daniel O'Connell was alive,
   When Daniel O'Connell was alive, to work upon the railway.
   Chorus

6. In eighteen hundred and forty-six, I changed my trade to carrying bricks.
   I changed my trade to carrying bricks, to work upon the railway.
   Chorus

7. In eighteen hundred and forty-seven, poor Paddy was thinking of going to heaven.
   Poor Paddy was thinking of going to heaven, to work upon the railway.
   Chorus

8. In eighteen hundred and forty-eight, I learnt to take my whiskey straight.
   I learnt to take my whiskey straight, to work upon the railway.
   Chorus

THE PARTING GLASS

Irish Folk Song

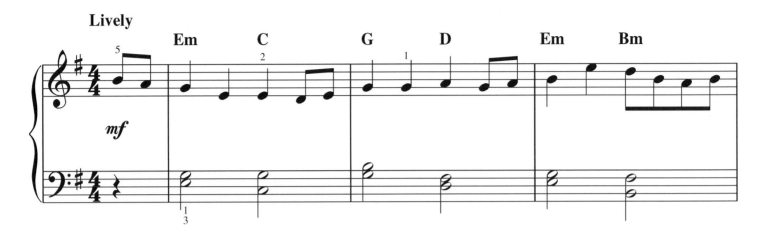

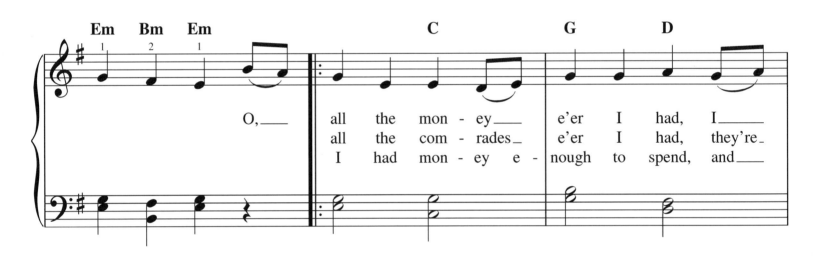

O,___ all the mon - ey___ e'er I had, I___
all the com - rades___ e'er I had, they're___
I had mon - ey e - nough to spend, and___

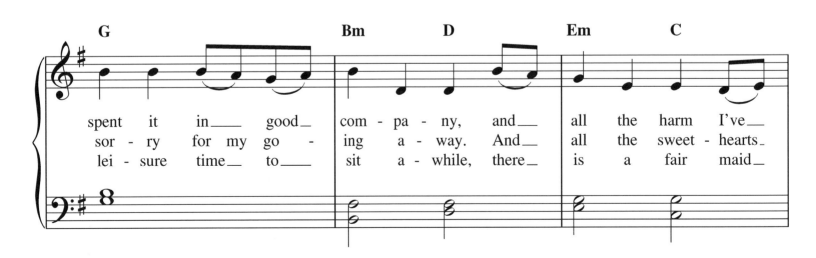

spent it in___ good___ com - pa - ny, and___ all the harm I've
sor - ry for my go - ing a - way. And___ all the sweet - hearts___
lei - sure time___ to___ sit a - while, there___ is a fair maid___

THE QUEEN OF CONNEMARA

Traditional Irish Folk Song

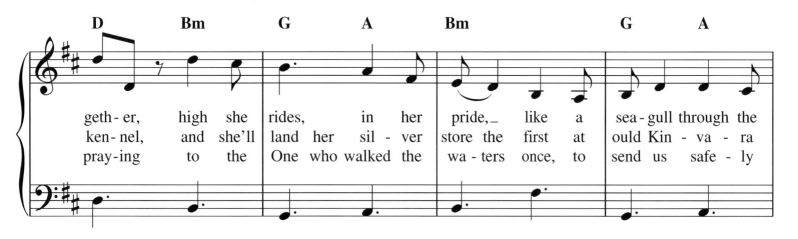

geth- er,   high she   rides,   in   her   pride,_   like   a   sea - gull through the
ken- nel,   and she'll   land her   sil - ver   store the   first   at   ould Kin - va - ra
pray-ing   to   the   One who walked the   wa - ters   once,   to   send us   safe - ly

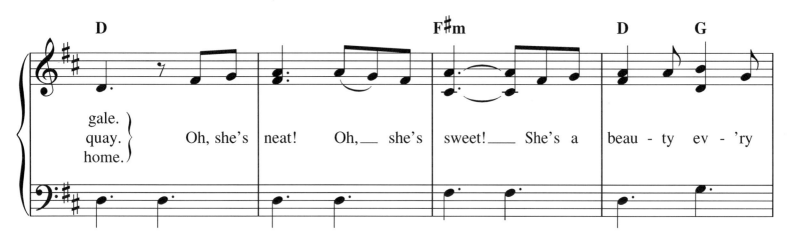

gale.
quay.   Oh, she's   neat!   Oh,_ she's   sweet!___ She's a   beau - ty ev - 'ry
home.

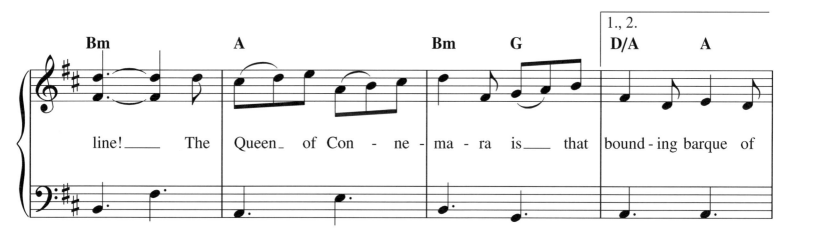

line!___   The   Queen_ of Con - ne - ma - ra is___ that   bound - ing barque of

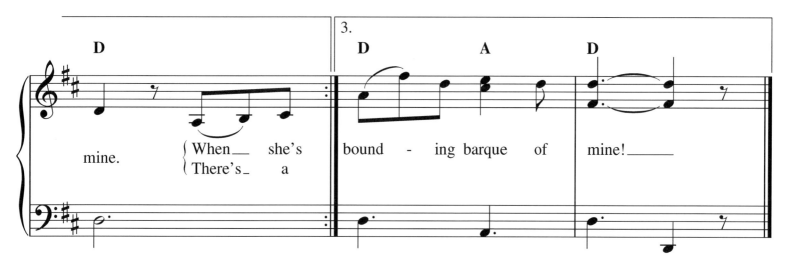

mine.   When_ she's   bound - ing barque of   mine!_____
There's_ a

THE RISING OF THE MOON

Traditional Irish Folk Song

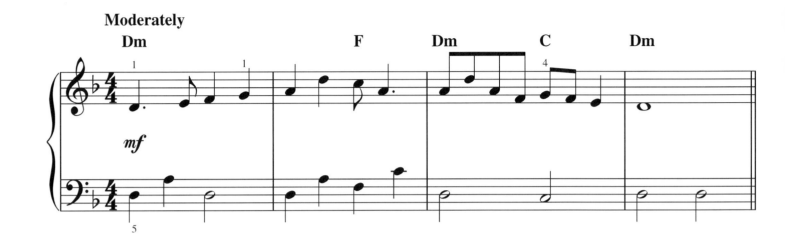

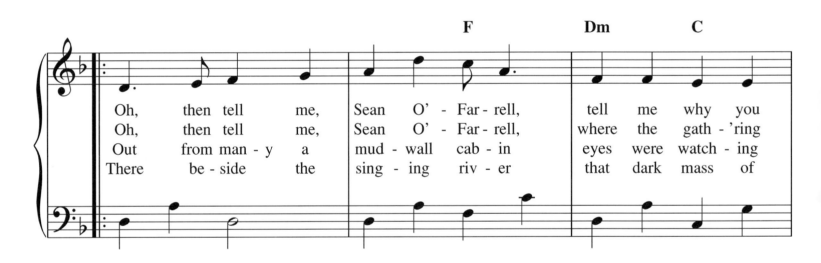

Oh, then tell me, Sean O' - Far - rell, tell me why you
Oh, then tell me, Sean O' - Far - rell, where the gath - 'ring
Out from man - y a mud - wall cab - in eyes were watch - ing
There be - side the sing - ing riv - er that dark mass of

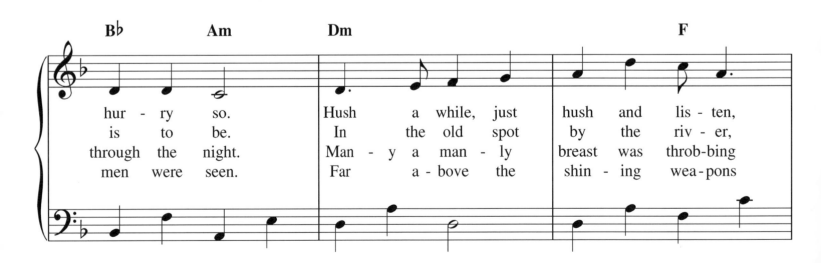

hur - ry so.
is to be.
through the night.
men were seen.

Hush a while, just
In the old spot
Man - y a man - ly
Far a - bove the

hush and lis - ten,
by the riv - er,
breast was throb - bing
shin - ing wea - pons

STAR OF COUNTY DOWN

Traditional Irish Folk Song

THE ROCKY ROAD TO DUBLIN

Traditional Irish Folk Song

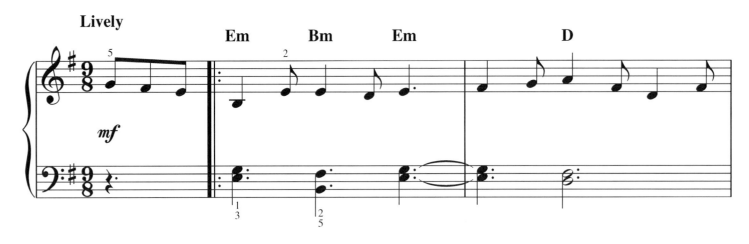

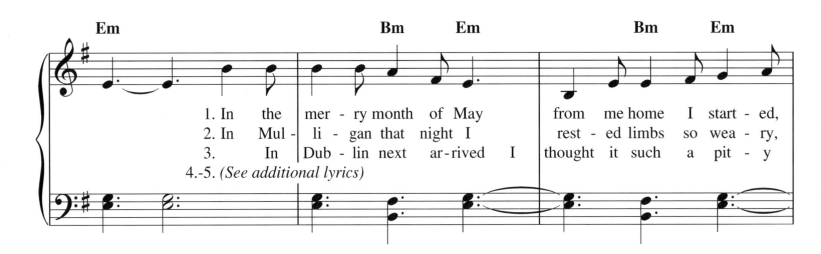

1. In the mer-ry month of May   from me home I start-ed,
2. In Mul-li-gan that night I   rest-ed limbs so wea-ry,
3. In Dub-lin next ar-rived I   thought it such a pit-y

4.-5. *(See additional lyrics)*

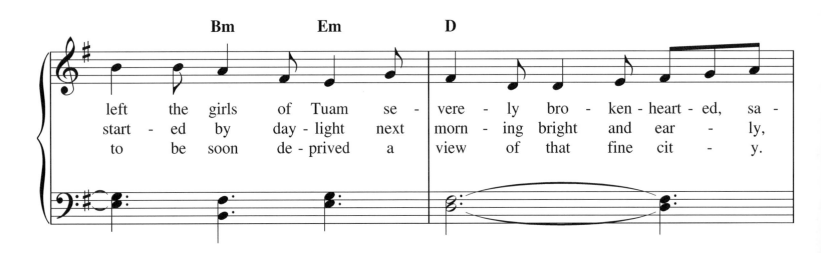

left the girls of Tuam se-ver-ly bro-ken-heart-ed, sa-
start-ed by day-light next morn-ing bright and ear-ly,
to be soon de-prived a view of that fine cit-y.

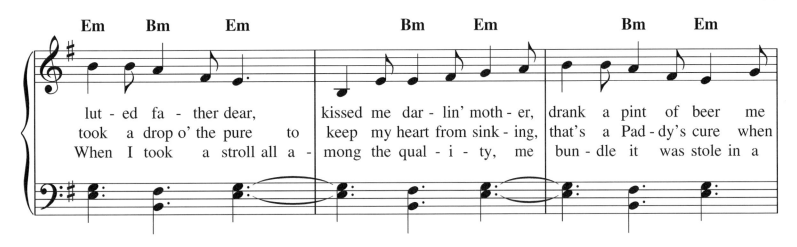

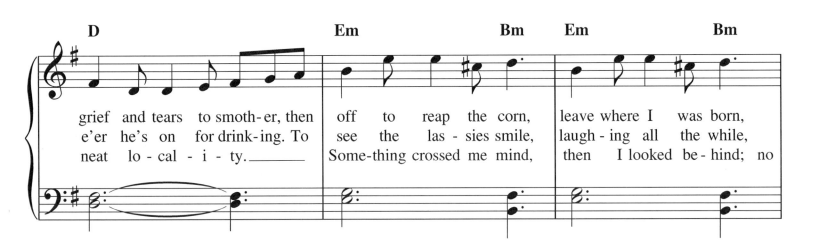

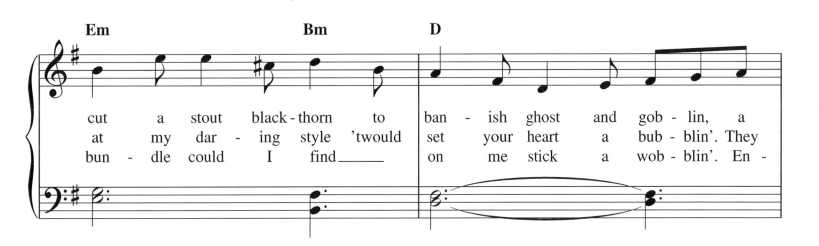

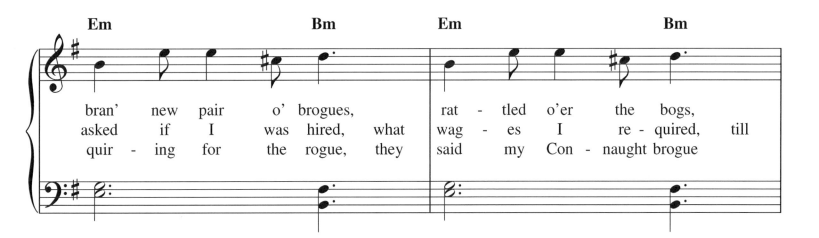

Additional Lyrics

4. From there I got away, me spirits never failing,
Landed on the quay as the ship was sailing.
Captain at me roared, said that no room had he,
When I jumped aboard, a cabin for Paddy.
Down among the pigs, I played some funny rigs,
Danced some hearty jigs, the water 'round me bubblin'.
When off Holyhead I wished meself was dead,
Or better far instead, on the rocky road to Dublin.
Chorus

5. The boys of Liverpool, when we safely landed,
Called meself a fool; I could no longer stand it.
Blood began to boil, temper I was losing,
Poor old Erin's Isle they began abusing.
"Hurrah, me boys," says I, shillelagh I let fly;
Some Galway boys were by and saw I was a-hobblin'.
Then with loud "Hurrah!" they joined in the affray
And quickly paved the way for the rocky road to Dublin.
Chorus